Forgotten Edens

This first edition belongs to

Morrison 3/93

Name *Date*

A *black lemur raises itself on a limb in a Madagascar forest.*

FORGOTTEN

EDENS

Exploring the World's Wild Places

Photographic Essays by Frans Lanting
Text Essays by Christine K. Eckstrom

Prepared by the Book Division, National Geographic Society, Washington, D.C.

FORGOTTEN EDENS
Exploring the World's Wild Places

Photographic essays by Frans Lanting
Text essays by Christine K. Eckstrom

Published by The National Geographic Society
Gilbert M. Grosvenor,
President and Chairman of the Board
Michela A. English, *Senior Vice President*

Prepared by The Book Division
William R. Gray, *Vice President and Director*
Margery G. Dunn, Charles Kogod,
Assistant Directors

Staff for this book
John G. Agnone, *Project Editor and Illustrations Editor*
Barbara A. Payne, *Text Editor*
Cinda Rose, *Art Director*
Barbara A. Payne, Penelope A. Timbers,
Researchers
Ron Fisher, *Consulting Editor*
Carl Mehler, *Map Research and Design*
Martin S. Walz, *Map Production*
Isaac Ortiz, *Map Relief*
Sandra F. Lotterman, *Editorial Assistant*
Artemis S. Lampathakis,
Illustrations Assistant
Heather Guwang,
Production Project Manager
Lewis R. Bassford, H. Robert Morrison,
Richard S. Wain, *Production*

Karen F. Edwards, Elizabeth G. Jevons,
Teresita Cóquia Sison, Karen Dufort Sligh,
Marilyn J. Williams, *Staff Assistants*

Elisabeth MacRae-Bobynskyj, *Indexer*

Manufacturing and Quality Management
George V. White, *Director;* John T. Dunn,
Associate Director; Vincent P. Ryan,
Manager; and R. Gary Colbert

Library of Congress CIP Data: page 199

PRECEDING PAGES: Elephants gather at a water hole in northern Botswana.

On Hawaii's Midway atoll, a female Laysan

albatross preens her mate as part of an extensive courtship ritual.

A *flying lizard extends ribbed membranes to glide through the tropical forest of* Borneo.

Morning fog lifts over the lowland rain forest of the Danum Valley region in northern Borneo.

Foreword

Almost every culture has a myth about a place of origin where people lived innocently in a pristine land. The most famous, perhaps, appears in the Bible as Eden—the garden paradise God created for Adam and Eve, located, some say, between the Tigris and the Euphrates Rivers, one of the most fertile regions of the ancient Middle East. That land once supported a great diversity of wildlife, from lions and tigers to herds of gazelles and wild cattle, but it became overpopulated by humans and overgrazed by their livestock, and is no longer a place to which we turn our attention when we go in search of earth's living Edens.

In our careers, we have both spent much of the past 15 years looking for last Edens, for those places that have escaped environmental degradation and reveal what nature is capable of on a grand scale. But our wanderings have taught us that even the most remote locations on earth now bear some mark of the modern world, and that no place is truly untouched any more by human endeavors.

So do Edens still exist? Yes and no. In the bewildering tropical rain forests of northern Borneo, we were awed by what we found, and we left with concern for the future of species not only unstudied but unnamed, on an island whose forests are being rapidly logged. The great aggregations of seabirds and marine mammals on the sub-Antarctic island of South Georgia, by contrast, are returning to a state of grace after being ravaged for more than a century. Hawaii's far atolls and remnant pockets of rain forest remind us of what the islands were like before introduced flora and fauna took an irreversible toll on native life. Madagascar's unique creatures face a threat all too common in our world, the loss of habitat without which many may not survive much longer. The Okavango Delta is an oasis of hope in a continent beset by environmental woes, but the temptation of its waters in a desert land and the economic potential of its wildlife resources present conservation questions that cannot be ignored.

Our goal with this book is to represent the glory and vitality of these last wild places without denying that they have been altered by human impact. That they are among the least changed makes them all the more precious and miraculous. But their survival cannot be left to chance. Isolation has been the most important factor in their persistence as separate worlds that few knew existed. That alone will no longer save them. Our hope is that these great reservoirs of life will inspire a new concept of Eden: We are no longer innocent; they are no longer pristine; but there is still time to make a new covenant.

Frans Lanting
Christine K. Eckstrom

BORNEO
The Infinite Tapestry

Along the banks of the Danum (overleaf), a wild river in northern Borneo where virgin rain forest rises majestically like the skyline of a big city, I was an astonished observer of the life within. Exploring on foot, I treasured rare encounters of the exotic kind, with a frilled lizard (below) poised on a giant leaf and a Yoda look-alike known as a tarsier (following pages).

Nearly invisible, a katydid clings to the underside of a leaf.

The Pale Rim Around Her Wings

In the night she was almost eaten by a tarsier. It was late evening, but she still rested where she had hidden all day, concealed along the midrib of a leaf. She's a katydid, and her body, luscious green and veined like a tender new leaf, is a perfect disguise for avoiding capture by day. Even the pale rim around her wings helps to compensate for any shadow her body might cast that could guide a hungry bird or lizard to her. In the cover of night she feeds on leaves and listens. The rain forest around her is so dark that you would not see that the trees rise 20 stories above her, but you might feel that the canopy reached even higher into the sky by the sheer volume of sound pulsing inside the forest. Wild trills and shrieks, piping bells and low hoo-oos overlie the steady rasping and buzzing and deep rhythmic thrum that comes from every layer of the forest. Through the shrill whines of mole crickets, the metallic clinks of tree frogs, and the swelling chirrs of unfathomable numbers of insects, she heard a male katydid singing. She picked up his song with tiny hearing organs on the joints of her forelegs. He was calling for a mate, and she responded. She crept to the tip of her leaf and waved her forelegs to home in on his position. Just above her sat a young male tarsier, a primate the size of a human hand. He clung to a sapling, his papery ears perked out like sails to the wind, his giant eyes open wide to see through the darkness. He sensed her movement, spun his gaze to her leaf, and sprang, but she flew just in time, a sudden whir swallowed up in the great drone of the night.

The symphony of cries surrounding the katydid speaks to the extravagance of life in her rain forest home. She lives deep in the lowlands of Borneo, the huge island that forms the lush, green heart of the Malay Archipelago. Shaped like a big ragged raindrop, Borneo straddles the Equator between Southeast Asia and Australia. It is the third largest island in the world, filling an area the size of the eastern United States. Politically, Borneo is shared by Indonesia and Malaysia, with the tiny nation of Brunei wedged along the northwest coast. Geographically, the island is fringed with mangrove-and-palm swamps and the mouths of rivers that snake inland through towering rain forests. From the coastal lowlands, the land rumples and rises to a mile-high central plateau, the headwaters of all the big rivers. In the far north, one lone, magnificent peak—Kinabalu—stands 13,455 feet above the sea of forests below, the highest mountain in Southeast Asia.

Ecologically, the island of Borneo is a center of biological richness for the Indo-Malayan region—and a hot spot of world biodiversity. Twenty-five acres of

Bornean rain forest can hold more species of trees than occur in all of North America. Borneo shelters more varieties of birds than are found in Europe and as many mammal species as live on the continent of Australia. For reptiles and amphibians, the statistics are equally high; but for insects, the figures are staggering. They comprise literally millions of species, of which only a minuscule percentage has been described by science. In Borneo, the little katydid symbolizes both the complexity and the mystery of the rain forest, whose entire fabric is an infinite tapestry of connections among species like hers. And while we may speculate on her ecology, based on what is known of other katydids, the one that whirled off into the night's black maw has not yet even been named.

The forest that sustains such a wealth of life has the stature of a great cathedral. The tallest trees in the Bornean rain forest soar to heights of 220 feet, higher than trees in Amazonia and Africa. They are the emergents, and they spread their boughs above the undulating roof of the forest canopy, open to the force of the sun and the wind. Most of the emergents and canopy trees are members of a family known as the dipterocarps, a word meaning "two-winged seed," which the

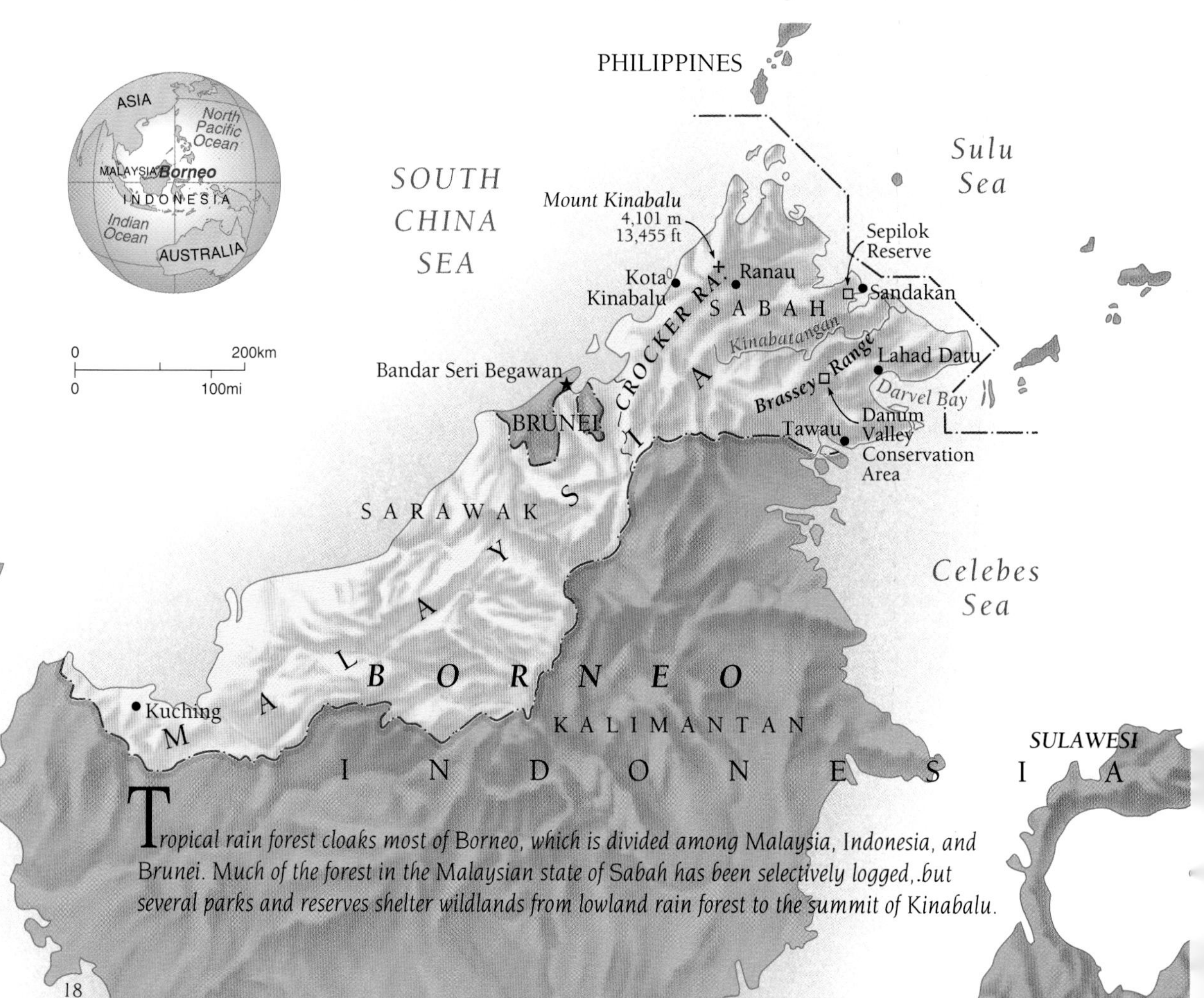

Tropical rain forest cloaks most of Borneo, which is divided among Malaysia, Indonesia, and Brunei. Much of the forest in the Malaysian state of Sabah has been selectively logged,.but several parks and reserves shelter wildlands from lowland rain forest to the summit of Kinabalu.

trees produce in periodic flushes, filling the forest with showers of brown whirligig seeds. They fall like swirls of spinning maple-leaf pods in the spring, drifting down through a world that is bathed in a pale green, perpetual twilight. Only 2 percent of the sunlight that shines on the canopy filters down to the forest floor. From the lacy boughs of the highest trees down to the great buttress roots that support them, the forest is layered with dense tiers of vegetation that shelter creatures both strange and magnificent. It is a world where giant squirrels overshadow tiny mouse deer twelve inches tall and delicate moths patterned like Indonesian batiks float by on nine-inch wings. Through the dark halls of the forest roam two-horned rhinoceroses; white-bibbed sun bears with shiny black fur; and sleek clouded leopards that stalk the night. There are bearded pigs, barking deer, scaly pangolins, and white moon rats that emerge like pale ghosts after dark. Through the trees flit broadbills the color of emeralds; brilliant pittas jeweled in garnet and blue; and hornbills with huge upcurved casques on their bills that work the canopy with lasso-whip wingbeats. High up swing solitary orangutans and troops of sociable gibbons, whose liquid, bubbling songs ring through the forest at dawn. There are bushy binturongs with prehensile tails; and along the rivers, proboscis monkeys with pendulous noses and partially webbed feet. There are insects that look like twigs; horned frogs that resemble dead leaves; and exquisite flower mantises precisely formed like the petals of an orchid—a disguise to their predators and a lure for the nectar-loving insects they eat.

The generous rains and constant warmth of the tropics create the steamy conditions that promote such a luxuriance of growth and life-forms. Monsoon winds sweep the warm seas around Borneo, bringing as much as 200 inches of rainfall to the island each year. Rain is the lifeblood of the forest, and even in the driest months, few weeks pass without showers—or the tension and release of a storm. It begins with a rumble like distant drums. The skies darken, and inside the forest it feels like nightfall. You hear the rain before it arrives. It sounds like a great ocean wave is approaching, and if you're near a clearing, you might see a broad gauzelike curtain sweeping toward you across the forest. The rain pummels the canopy and streams to the forest floor. It teems down on the rivers with a thunderous beat and turns steep trails into rushing waterways. Then suddenly it slows and stops. Sunlight beams down on the canopy. The forest drips, gleaming with moisture, and the world seems at once breathless and renewed.

On a bough high above the forest floor, two eyes bulge up. With a hop, a big frog lands on top of the branch. It's just after dark, and one hundred feet down, raindrops from the leaves of small saplings are still plinking into a pool. It's a wallow created by a rhino, whose regular visits there to roll in the mud keep it a sump of shallow water. In a subtle way, the life of the delicate green frog is bound to the habits of the lumbering gray rhino: The heavy rains that soak the forest are quickly absorbed, and standing water is scarce. The frog is a female, and though she spends most of her life in the trees, she has to lay her eggs in a nest overhanging still water so that her tadpoles can drop in and grow into frogs.

When she's ready to breed, she and her mate must journey down from the canopy to a pool on the forest floor, and that time is now. The male is already there. Far below her, he sits by the wallow and sings. She looks down, inches forward, and leaps. Her feet snap open like fans, and on outstretched webs connecting each finger and toe, she flies. Free-falling like a tiny parachute, she glides in a graceful, slow-curving spiral, down through the dizzying heights of the forest, and lands on a broad leaf with a plop.

She is known as a Wallace's flying frog, for the 19th-century naturalist Alfred Russel Wallace, who first described her, and her astonishing aerial ability is believed to be linked to the unusual architecture of the Bornean forest. The canopy is more uneven than those in Amazonia and Africa; it rises and falls in rolling

waves, with huge emergents poking up like islands. Beneath the canopy, the tall trees often branch high up; there are fewer lianas twining among the trunks, and travel between and across levels of the forest is not as smooth for the creatures of Borneo as for those of other rain forests. To get where she needs to go, the frog flies—and she is not alone. One of the singularly amazing features of the Bornean forest is the wild array of animals that have adapted to the forest's structure with gliding flight. There are giant flying squirrels and so-called flying lemurs, which spread huge elastic membranes connecting their legs to soar like dark kites between trees. There are flying lizards with red-and-yellow-patterned wings on their sides; flying geckos, which spread sucker-tipped webbed feet and skin flaps tucked under their bellies to sail between boughs; and perhaps most

Polished by glaciers, Mount Kinabalu rises thousands of feet above the forests of Borneo.

B*orneo's jungle is cleared for human endeavors such as this palm oil plantation in Sabah.*

remarkable of all, flying snakes, which flatten their ribs and extend narrow folds of skin along the length of their bodies to swim through the air in fast, squiggling S-curves, drifting down through the layers of the forest.

The wind rustles the canopy, and a leaf twirls down to the forest floor. Within six weeks' time, it will have returned to the canopy—decayed and reabsorbed as nutrients taken up by the sprawling roots of the great trees. One of the surprising twists of the rain forest's richness is the poverty of the soil that anchors such a kingdom of life: Ninety-five percent of the organic nutrients of the Bornean forest are above ground, in the forest itself. The showers of leaves, animal droppings, blossoms, and fruits that steadily rain down from the canopy layers are recycled many tens of times faster than in temperate forests; otherwise, their nutrients would be flushed away by the rains.

The forest floor is the musty workplace of the great decomposers and recyclers of the rain forest—fungi and bacteria, beetles and millipedes, ants and termites—and if you hike into the forest after an evening shower, some of them reveal their works in wondrous ways. Wait until dusk, when the six-o'clock cicadas begin to whine and geckos bark from the trees; watch until darkness has risen like black fog from the floor of the forest to the sky. Enter the forest with a flashlight, alone and silent, then stand motionless and turn off the light. Beneath

your feet and all through the undergrowth, the ground twinkles with chips of silver. It seems you are standing on a fallen drapery of phosphorescent lace. The sparkling chips are luminescent fungi, and their weird light shines from the leaves and twigs on which they are feeding. Underground, fungi spread fine threads like roots, penetrating organic debris and slowly breaking it down. Especially after a good rain, their fruiting bodies appear—mushrooms and toadstools and other fungi shaped in the bizarre forms of undersea tree corals, hairy orange cups, and delicate snow-white veils. Nearby on a rotting log, a fresh cluster of mushrooms sprouts up and glows fluorescent green, casting an eerie nimbus like pale neon. Chemicals in certain fungi make them gleam in the dark—some with a light so bright that you can carry them as a faint torch in the forest. Their luminescence may be a beacon to the beetles and other creatures of the night that consume them and spread their spores through the forest.

By morning, the green mushrooms have disappeared; a lone beetle creeps down the old log. The leaf litter rustles, and a tiny, pointed nose pokes up. A furry, brown creature rushes over the log—and the beetle is gone, carried off in a skittering zip through the leaves. The shadowy form is a treeshrew, a small mammal that looks like a fluffy-tailed squirrel, with a long conical snout, black glass-button eyes, and naked ears like a little monkey's. Like squirrels, bats, civets, and other small mammals, treeshrews play a key role in dispersing the seeds of the Bornean forest; but their movements are so swift and secretive that at best they are only glimpsed. Though you might not spot the female that raced off with the beetle, you can sense her presence by a musky scent. Often in the forest you smell creatures you never see. The air is so humid and still that the odors of animals and the fragrances of fruits and blossoms linger in unseen clouds, and sometimes you seem to pass through spheres of scent that let you know what may be near. The treeshrew leaves a trail of scent wherever she goes, marking her territory; and if you could follow her crazed paths through the forest, you would see that once every other morning she slips off at first light to a particular tree. Each time, she takes a new route, jumping between different saplings to make her approach. Fifteen feet up, she pauses on a bough by the tree, silent and motionless, then jumps into a hole in the trunk. Inside lie two newborn treeshrews, nestled in a bed of leaves. The babies nurse eagerly, swelling into fat balls full of milk. Then the mother climbs out and springs off, not to return for two days. In her absence the young ones' survival seems to rest on immobility and silence, and one other defense: The baby treeshrews have almost no scent.

Like most animals of the Bornean forest, the treeshrew is solitary, and she

At the Sepilok Reserve, a warden oversees the care of orangutans being restored to the wild.

logs the daily equivalent of a marathon—running for as much as ten hours a day over a relatively huge territory of several acres, just to find what she needs to survive. Her solitariness and hard work point to a paradox of what seems so fruitful and beneficent an environment. The forest holds immense varieties of plants and animals, but most are widely scattered. Competition in the forest is intense for space, light, water, and food—and among plants, for pollinators and dispersers of seeds. Many plants have developed specialized relationships with other species. The intricate designs of most orchid blossoms fit hand in glove with specific insect pollinators; some trees produce fabulous blooms and cascades of fruits directly from their trunks to accommodate feeders and pollinators that inhabit the understory layers; and certain species of shrubs known as ant plants exude secretions that nourish private armies of ants that live in hollow chambers inside their stems and ferociously defend the plants against other insects that might destroy them. But of all the floral forms in the Bornean forest, one stands forth as the most outrageous—the incredible flower known as the rafflesia. From a distance, a rafflesia in full bloom looks like a brilliant red-and-white spaceship that has just touched down on the forest floor. From a huge opening at the center of the blossom, five gigantic petals fan out, spanning a width that can exceed three feet. It is the largest flower in the world. The petals are thick and leathery to the touch—colored in a garish crimson-orange and often nubbled with bright white spots—and amid the browning leaves and debris of the forest floor, the flower looks so flamboyant and excessively designed that it seems like a science-fiction creation.

The 16 species of rafflesia are native to Southeast Asia; many are unique to Borneo and extremely rare. Their requirements for survival are both exacting and mysterious. Rafflesia is actually a parasite. The plant body consists solely of tiny filaments, like a fungus, that live only inside one particular vine, *Tetrastigma,* an unremarkable-looking member of the grape family. No one knows how a rafflesia seed germinates and grows; it first appears as a thimble-size

brown bud on the grapevine that over a year's time steadily swells. In the biggest species, it expands to the size of a soccer ball. Then, on some unknown cue, the petals unfold like gigantic frilled, red lips around the flower's gaping mouth.

If it's nearby, you can usually find your way to a blooming rafflesia—even in the thick tangle of the forest floor. Just after opening, most rafflesia blossoms send forth an odor as tremendous as the flower itself. The smell is like rotting flesh, and it is presumed to be a lure to the carrion flies that pollinate the flower. Within a few days after opening, the blossom withers and collapses in a dark, slimy mass. After that, its propagation hangs on a tenuous network of events: Only if the flower was a female, fertilized by pollen carried from a male blossom that opened at exactly the same time, will the rafflesia produce a fruit full of seeds; and until recently, no one knew how these were dispersed. One morning, from a blind set up near a ripe rafflesia fruit, scientists observed a small, dark creature climb into the fruit to feed. It was a treeshrew, and it ate for several minutes, then scampered off—the top of its nose covered with pulp.

One place where rafflesia still thrives is on the lower slopes of Mount Kinabalu, the massive peak that rises like a glorious mountain island within the island of Borneo itself. All across northern Borneo, Kinabalu draws the eye. Sometimes heavy wreaths of clouds so completely encircle its base that it seems to float alone in the sky. The illusion befits the mountain: Kinabalu is a separate world, both linked to the tropical forests from which it rises and unique unto itself. From the lowland rain forests that wrap the base of the mountain to the 13,000-foot heights of the summit plateau, the slopes of Kinabalu are layered with distinct zones of life. Above the high-tide line of the lowland rain forests, at about 4,000 feet, more than half of the plants on the mountain are Kinabalu's own—found nowhere else in the world.

Climbing the mountain is an Alice-in-Wonderland experience, as you hike through awesome colonnades of lowland dipterocarps into a montane zone of oaks and chestnuts, myrtles and laurels—their branches decked with sprays of orchids. Of Borneo's more than 3,000 orchid species—10 percent of the world's total—more than 1,200 varieties grow on Kinabalu. Higher in the cloud forest, you climb through thick stands of bamboos and tree ferns that glisten with moisture combed from the clouds; then up to groves of stunted trees, whose gnarled boughs are spongy with mosses and laden more thickly with even tinier orchids.

Above 8,000 feet the trees grow ever thinner and smaller, and the soil is so exceedingly poor that few species can survive the twin rigors of cold and lack of nutrients. But here one of Kinabalu's most celebrated families of plants has moved into an impoverished ecological niche—and flourished. They are known as pitcher plants, and they have adapted to the harsh conditions with one of the most curious features of the plant kingdom: As they grow, some of their leaf tips uncurl and swell into long, bulbous hollows, with flaps that pop open like old-fashioned water pitchers with hinged lids. In different species the pitchers assume a wild array of shapes—from the wasp-waisted Low's pitcher, colored in lime green with a flaring burgundy mouth, to the gigantic Rajah, whose dark crimson urn can hold more than a quart of liquid. They dangle from boughs, swaying in the wind, and nestle along the steep slopes like displays of painted pottery in an artist's studio window. But the pitchers are deadly lures: Under their rims they secrete a tempting nectar that attracts insects, which slip into a pool of digestive liquid and dissolve—supplying the pitchers with nutrients that the plants are believed to need to survive. As they age, their lids curl back, and the pitchers fill with rain; some animals come to drink from old pitchers, and if you look inside, you may see the larvae of freshly hatched insects, a cluster of snail's eggs, or a tiny black frog peeping to call a mate to the pitcher's pool.

Beyond the pitcher-plant zone, the trees and shrubs steadily shrink to knee height and lower. Great banks of clouds rush up the slopes; the winds gust hard, stinging with mist. At 11,000 feet you pass the tree line; and 2,000 feet higher up steep, naked rock spreads the summit plateau, a broad plain of granite cracked and peeled by ice and heat, and ringed with a dozen magnificent spires. If you climb to the summit of Kinabalu at sunrise, before the morning clouds build to engulf the mountain, you can see westward to the pale blue mirror of the South China Sea and look south across ridge after ridge of lowland rain forest below. But the view is different from what a climber would have seen even 30 years ago. More people are settled in the valleys below; in the clearing season you can see tall columns of smoke rising from the fields they are burning. Tiny red lines wind through the forested hills beyond, and if you could glide down and fly over the canopy like a hornbill, you could follow trucks rumbling down the red dirt roads, their trailers piled high with giant logs.

The face of Borneo is changing fast. The dipterocarp trees that form the great pillars of the forest are the most commercially valuable tropical hardwoods in Southeast Asia; throughout Borneo they are rapidly being logged. The sale of their timber fuels the economies of Malaysian and Indonesian Borneo, and most of the island's lowland dipterocarp forests have been, or are scheduled to be, logged. The majority of the cutting is selective—few forests have been clear-cut—but the impact is more complex than the mere removal of the largest trees.

Critics say that the act of felling and hauling often destroys swaths of surrounding forest and that the presence of logging operations, in many places, disrupts local communities' traditional use of the forest. Others point out that the logging roads that vein the forest offer easy access for hunters and poachers and open new lands to clearing by settlers. While studies have shown that most mammals and birds can survive in carefully managed logged forests, some have requirements too precise to survive logging's effects. For the many plants and animals that live only in virgin forest—and the countless creatures whose associations with other species form the forest's grand interlocking web of life—a tree falls, and their world goes with it.

But a climber standing atop Mount Kinabalu would not be able to see other significant changes of the past 30 years. Most of the land visible from the summit is part of the Malaysian state of Sabah, and since 1964, when the first park was established around Kinabalu, more areas have been designated for protection. Southwest of Kinabalu stretches the long spine of the Crocker Range, an entire mountain chain that is now a national park. To the east, a vital habitat along the Kinabatangan River has been proposed as a park to protect the rare proboscis monkeys, which live in the mangrove-and-palm forests along its shores. On an especially clear day on Kinabalu you might even see far to the southeast, to a region of lowland rain forest known as the Danum Valley Conservation Area. Though it covers only 170 square miles, Danum Valley is the largest protected area of virgin lowland rain forest in northern Borneo, and it holds a sample of one of the richest natural kingdoms on earth, from rhinos and leaf monkeys, argus pheasants and otter civets, to tiny treeshrews and flying frogs—even the tarsier and the small green katydid.

At dawn, the morning mist rises like steam from the huge lowland trees along the banks of the Danum River: The forest is breathing. By early evening the rain forest seems to exhale the very darkness it holds within, and far away to the northwest, when the last light gilds the highest rocks of Kinabalu, the blackness in the lowlands is already complete. Deep in the forest where the katydid lives, the insects are screaming. A family of flying squirrels glides the night skies across the river, and farther down in the dense understory the little tarsier has just awakened. His eyes open wide and round to drink in the secret motions of the darkness. He leaps between saplings and freezes, muscles tensed—he's hungry tonight. Every feature of his being is designed for the nighttime hunt—powerful legs for jumping; sucker pads on his fingers and toes for clinging; huge radar ears for detecting the slightest sound. But it's his eyes that are truly extraordinary: They are 150 times bigger in relation to his size than are ours. He spins his head fast—a full 180 degrees—and fixes his stare on something below. The green katydid inches forward from the midrib of her leaf, directly into his sight line. The tarsier springs, and this time he doesn't miss. In a blink in the darkness, she is gone. But hidden in the leaves below, her eggs are nearly ready to hatch.

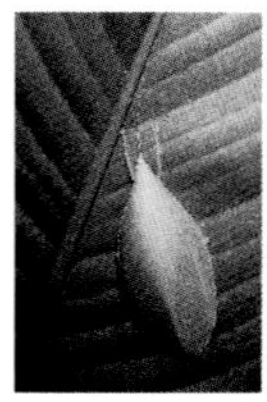

Looking for animals in the dimly lit underworld of a Bornean *jungle is like trying to remember scenes from a dream.* Even *when they're within reach, they remain elusive, and a clear view rarely materializes.* From *fleeting glimpses* I *constructed impressions of existences more imagined than experienced.* Peering *out from behind a giant tree buttress, a nocturnal civet (above) is ready to slink away into darkness.* Caked *with mud from a wallow, one of* Sabah's *last rhinos (opposite) raises an eye that meets mine for an instant, before it vanishes into the undergrowth.*

Mirror images of the world in which they evolved, a horned toad (opposite) moves inconspicuously across leaf litter; and a gauzy bush cricket flattens itself into imperceptibility on a tree trunk. In utter contrast, a three-foot-wide rafflesia flower (following pages) is impossible to overlook; its tiny pollinator, a carrion fly, is lured not by the blossom's size but by a foul odor like that of a decaying carcass.

*H*overing in a helicopter over the forest, I noticed that the canopy is less interlocked than in Amazonia or Africa, a feature that some say has contributed to the rise of a fauna unique in the world. Flying has become an easier way to travel for an unlikely array of creatures ranging from geckos and snakes to lizards and frogs. Rana pardalis (*following pages*), a tiny cousin of the famous flying frog first described by naturalist Alfred Russel Wallace, stretches all four fanned feet to extend its controlled glide.*

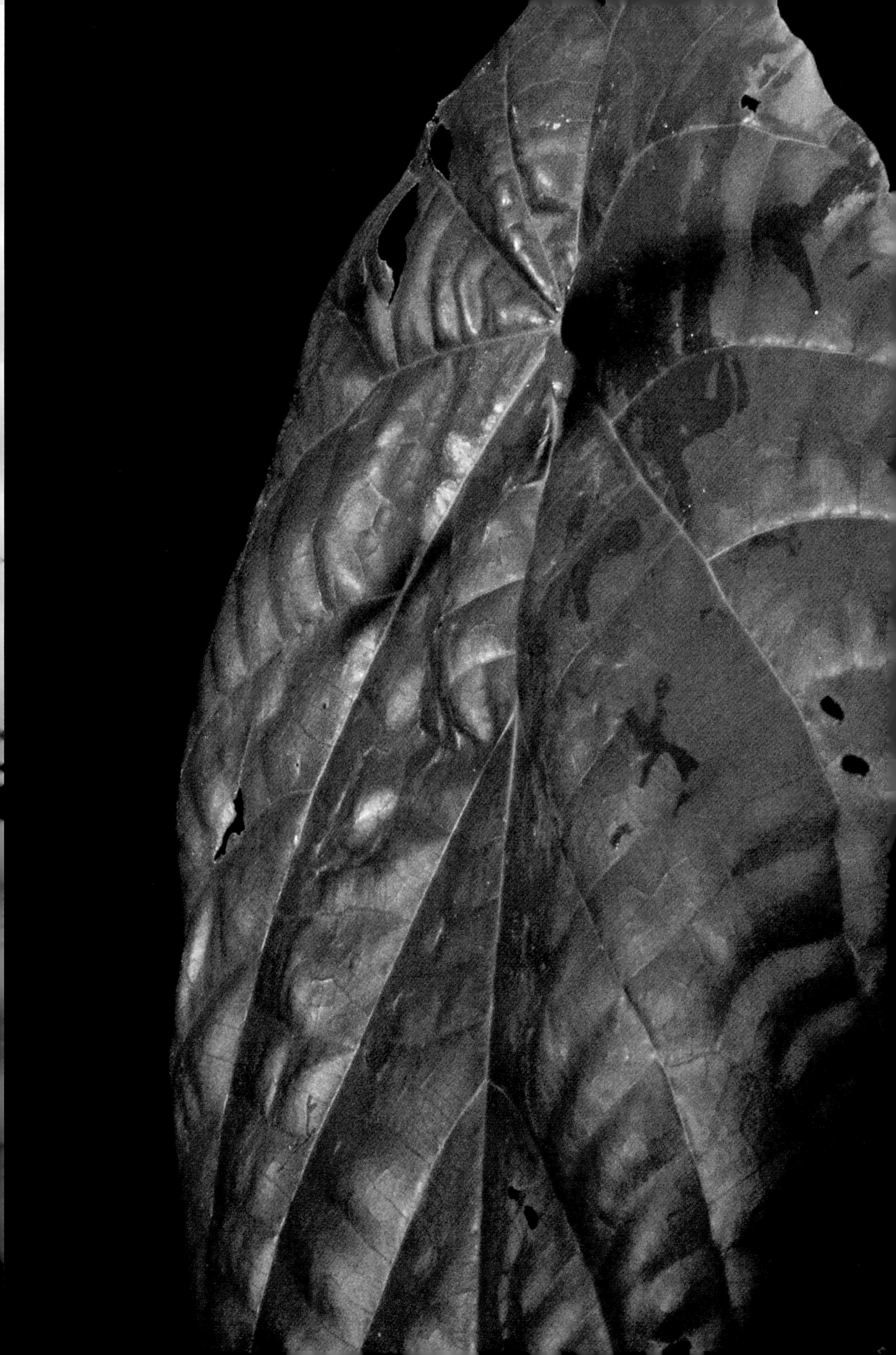

The stylized defense posture of an unnamed leaf insect may startle a lesser enemy but would not faze a formidable foe like the greater treeshrew, a squirrel-size enigma that is neither purely arboreal nor insectivorous like a shrew. Once considered primitive primates, treeshrews are now classed in their own order; most occur in Borneo.

Time and again the wonder of the forest's intricate connections revealed itself when I took time to study the details. I marveled at the life of an unnamed mite, which glued its larvae to a daddy longlegs. Inside cup fungi (opposite)—each the size of a fingernail—I saw spore packets designed to be dispersed by the impact of waterdrops dripping from the canopy.

F*ound only in* Borneo, *the leaf-eating proboscis monkey is rapidly headed for extinction because of the fragmentation of its coastal mangrove forest; but a proposed new park along* Sabah's Kinabatangan River, *where the largest surviving population lives, may be a last respite for the biggest monkey of* Southeast Asia. Near *the river,* I *watched from a small boat as an adult male measured and took his leap across a tributary lined with nipa palms.* Other *times, it was hard to remain a detached observer whenever* I *saw the monkeys fall short and land in the river with whopping belly flops.*

Pitcher plants are renowned as insect traps; less known is how they serve the needs of other organisms. Some snails negotiate spikes inside a pitcher to lay their eggs (left). Other pitchers (below) become water reservoirs for animals—once rain dilutes the enzymes inside the cups. The large ant on a pitcher plant (opposite) has yet to be found inside as a victim; its relationship with the plant is a mystery.

I admired the unhurried confidence of orangutans as they moved high through the trees (opposite), selecting branches strong enough to support their considerable weight and engaging in playful acrobatics a hundred feet in the air. Play was not on the mind of an adult male pig-tailed macaque (above) as he alternately watched a squabble among troop members and eyed my camera bags for edible contents.

After a month of rain, birds such as the paradise flycatcher (above) begin to nest. Other forest rhythms are not fully understood. Fig trees bear fruit unpredictably; when they do, green broadbills (below) join other creatures in a feeding frenzy. The whole forest is affected when dipterocarp trees burst into bloom (opposite), a phenomenon that occurs perhaps once a decade.

Like other great mountains such as Fuji *and* Kilimanjaro, Mount Kinabalu *dominates the landscape physically and spiritually; and it is hard to accept the geologic fact that this awesome granite outcrop rose just over a million years ago.* A *floral fortress,* Kinabalu's *flanks nurture one of the highest concentrations of unique plant life on earth—including a dazzling* 1,200 *species of orchids.*

SOUTH GEORGIA

On the Edge of Antarctica

On South Georgia Island, a lonely outpost of the Antarctic where icebergs float in frigid grandeur, I immersed myself in the daily drama of penguin societies (overleaf) and was a privileged observer of the awesome courtship of a wandering albatross (following pages) spreading ten-foot wings to a prospective mate.

In a landscape blanketed by a midsummer blizzard, a wandering albatross incubates its single egg.

To Ride the Black Gales of Winter

For a moment, the leaden skies that have made the day a long dusk break apart, and light passes over the land like a cloud. It pours across fields of tall tussock grasses, runs over the sea in a shimmering wave, and rolls up the far shore to reveal a great range of black mountains crowned with ice. It brightens the snows on the shoulders of the hills and illuminates the white feathers of a wandering albatross, seated in the golden tussock, shining like alabaster in the window of light. Then the skies close again and darken. A fresh squall rushes over the mountains, bringing a hard, cold rain. The winds increase, and the rain turns to sleet—blowing in stinging sheets over the grasses. By morning, snowfall blankets the land. In the field of tussock, the albatross sits, its position unchanged. It might seem the bird is huddled in place against the fury of the storm, lying low through the gales and swirls of the blizzard, but in fact the albatross is quite accustomed to the weather. It is midsummer on the sub-Antarctic island of South Georgia, the breeding season for seabirds of the southern ocean, and the albatross is incubating an egg.

In its stoic, snowy beauty the albatross is the supreme emblem of the land where it broods. Its nest is perched on a small islet off the coast of South Georgia, a 106-mile-long island that rises up like a wild rogue wave in the frigid reaches of the South Atlantic Ocean. The island lies at latitude 54 degrees south—in the "Furious 50s" of mariners' nightmares—where storm gusts regularly exceed 120 miles an hour and whip ocean swells to 50-foot heights. These are the only latitudes in which the wind and the ocean circle the globe unimpeded by continents, and they are home to many of the world's albatrosses, birds built for the storms and in love with the wind.

South Georgia is one of a scattering of small islands that ring Antarctica like the moons of an icy planet. Its location downwind and due east of the gale-beaten Drake Passage between South America and Antarctica brings South Georgia what has been called the worst weather on earth. Year-round successions of depressions and fronts, strengthened as they funnel between the continents, batter South Georgia's rough peaks, which spire to heights of nearly 10,000 feet. So dramatically does the island loom up from the sea that it has been described as "a stretch of the Alps in mid-ocean."

Much of the island is permanently covered in ice and snow, with much of the rest too sheer for either to take hold. Deep fjords cleave the mountains. Huge

A Weddell seal stares with curiosity at a visitor, perhaps the first human it's ever seen.

glaciers spill down from rocky slopes to the sea. Towering icebergs drift near the shores. Gale-force winds and sub-zero temperatures are recorded every month of the year, as are all forms of precipitation from mist to hail—sometimes several times in a single day. There are no native land mammals, no freshwater fish, and the climate is too cruel for most plants to survive. "Not a tree or shrub was to be seen, no not even big enough to make a tooth-pick," wrote the English explorer Capt. James Cook, the first to step ashore on South Georgia in 1775. He claimed it for Britain and sailed away, calling it "not . . . worth the discovery." One of his crew assessed South Georgia as "of less value than the smallest farmstead in England." Another felt "The very thought to live here a year fills the whole Soul with horror & despair."

Cook and his men had hoped to find a new continent, not a treeless isle. Even the scene that greeted them failed to soften their disappointment. They arrived in January, the height of the austral summer, a season when South Georgia's coasts and skies stream with unimaginable multitudes of mammals and birds. Hundreds of thousands of elephant seals, a million or more fur seals, more than six million penguins, and an array of seabirds in numbers exceeding 70 million all come in from the long night of the southern ocean winter to find their mates each spring on the island. For the seabirds and seals that ride the winds and waters around the wild white continent, South Georgia is the single most important nesting and breeding ground in the world, a haven in the high seas near the end of the earth.

The pack ice surrounding Antarctica booms. Deep cracks open up, the ice heaves and groans. Near the seaward edge, massive floes—some half the size of South Georgia—break free and surge north, driven by the powerful winds of the vernal equinox. From the darkness of midwinter on South Georgia, when the nights are 17 hours long, the days have steadily lengthened. The sun climbs higher now; the air grows a bit warmer. Inside a glacier high over the shore, a sudden fissure forks down like lightning, and a great ice wall falls to the ocean with a terrible thunder. Spring has arrived.

A dark form moves undersea off the coast. It grows larger as it nears the shore, then rolls in on a breaking wave and rears up. A huge head emerges, dripping with seawater, yawns open, and releases a roar. It is late August, early in the Southern Hemisphere spring, and the male elephant seal hauling up on the island is the first herald of the frenzied season about to begin. He's an old bull, judging by the length of his snout—the feature for which his species was named—and by his size, nearly 20 feet long, he probably weighs 4 tons. Soon after, other males come in, and for a week or two they jockey for position on the beach until one day the cows arrive. Thousands of females crawl up from the sea and the males go wild. With spectacular displays of rearing and roaring, bluff charges and gargled moans, the bulls vie to be beachmaster of a stretch of the shore and control a big harem of cows. They'll fight if they must, one on one, chest to chest, slashing and tearing with oversize canines, until the loser hobbles to the fringes of the colony, to loll with the young and the conquered.

Many of the females lumber in from the sea, heavy with young. They give birth within a few days and gather together in mounds like weathered boulders, lounging and sleeping, their pups growing fat on rich milk. The beachmaster sits tall among them, on guard. When the females are ready to breed again, he mates with his harem, all the while defending the challenges from fresh males coming in from the sea.

More dark forms appear in the waters. By mid-November they wash up in sleek waves on the shores. By the tens of hundreds of thousands they clamber up from the surf, gleaming brown masses of Antarctic fur seals. They too come now to bear young and breed, most returning to the same rookeries year after year, some to the very beaches where they were born. Among the noisy mobs, the big males posture and skirmish for territories, arching up, chests puffed, noses to the sky—pointing up to a blizzard of birds.

Wheeling in from all over the southern ocean soar tens of millions of seabirds, homing in on the towering ice isle. Petrels and prions, skuas and gulls, wandering albatrosses and Antarctic terns fill the skies with a mad, screaming chorus of cries as they wing in to nesting sites all over South Georgia. Then up from the sea come more birds. Huge flotillas of penguins spring onto the shores—macaronis and gentoos, kings and chinstraps—bounding out in black-and-white millions, some scrambling up steep cliffs, some waddling up the beaches, weaving around the vast shoals of seals.

It would not seem possible for so desolate a land to support such a massive invasion of life. But the influx of animals is seasonal, and none are creatures of

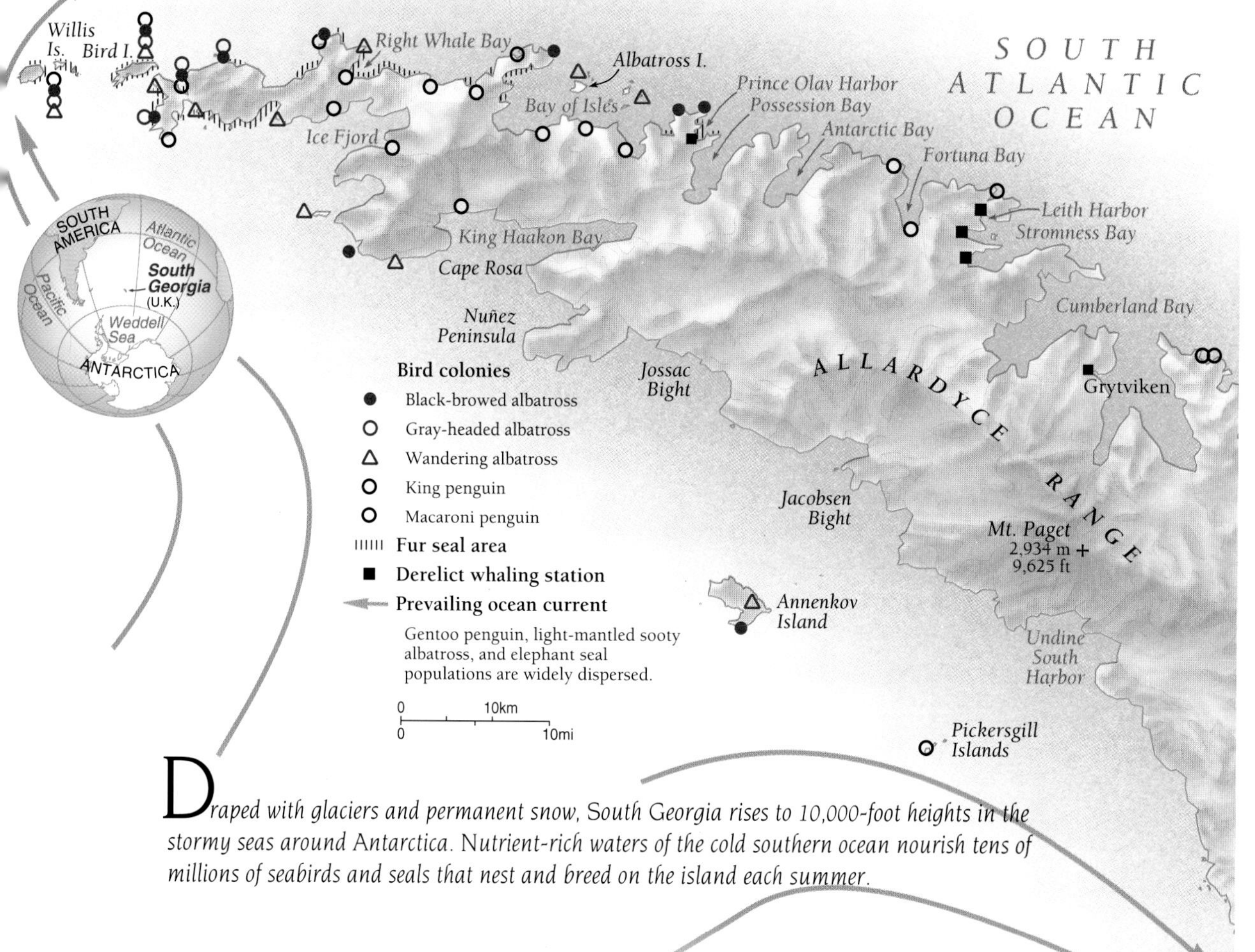

Draped with glaciers and permanent snow, South Georgia rises to 10,000-foot heights in the stormy seas around Antarctica. Nutrient-rich waters of the cold southern ocean nourish tens of millions of seabirds and seals that nest and breed on the island each summer.

the soil. All are migrants and marine—mammals and birds that live on the fat of the sea. In contrast to the paucity of resources on the island itself, the stormy plains of ocean around South Georgia are among earth's most productive waters.

Another ring encircles Antarctica, a physical boundary in the sea. Known as the Antarctic Convergence, it is a zone where the warmer waters of the Atlantic, Pacific, and Indian Oceans meet the frigid seas flowing around the ice continent. It defines the limits of the southern ocean with a sharp temperature change that serves as a biological frontier: The flora and fauna on one side differ from those on the other. The Convergence curves and sways around the globe like a permanent atmospheric front in the sea. Often from a ship it can be seen—a shifting line of foam on the surface, with flocks of seabirds swooping above, fishing the borders.

The southern ocean within the Convergence is so cold that temperate-zone creatures drifting into its waters rarely survive, but the few species adapted to its rigors occur in astounding numbers. The ocean's constant, near-freezing temperatures promote high concentrations of dissolved oxygen and nutrients that under the prolonged sunlight of the Antarctic summer nourish extraordinary blooms of phytoplankton—so dense they may tinge the ocean green. The phytoplankton sustain vast schools of krill, shrimplike crustaceans that are the hub of the Antarctic food web. Everything eats krill—squid and fish, penguins and seabirds, seals and whales. Many depend solely on krill to survive.

South Georgia lies within the Convergence, its long coast angled broadside to the prevailing currents sweeping west from the Drake Passage and spiraling north from the Weddell Sea. Geologically, the island is the tip of an undersea mountain range surrounded by a continental shelf, and as currents flow around its submarine plateau, complex mixings and upwellings bring a superabundant flush of sea life. Krill in multithousand-ton swarms have been recorded off South Georgia. Of all the isles that ring Antarctica within the ocean ring of the Convergence, South Georgia rises amid the lushest pastures of the southern ocean—and supports the richest Eden of life.

With subtle and specific strategies, the creatures that come to South Georgia have subdivided the island, the seas—even the months of the summer and the hours of the day—in ways that allow them all to thrive there at once. Seals crowd the beaches; penguins pepper the inland plains and steep rocky slopes; albatrosses nest on windy buttes and high cliffs; and the millions of petrels and prions make burrows among the tussock mounds. Rhythms within the communities of the more diminutive seabirds have a delicate precision: The blue petrels and dove prions—the most numerous birds on the island—both nest in tussock burrows, but breed at different times in the summer, while the two species of diving petrels, which both plunge-dive for krill, have different nesting sites, as well as staggered breeding seasons.

All the seals fast until the mating season is over, then they feast—but on different foods. Elephant seals dive for squid; special

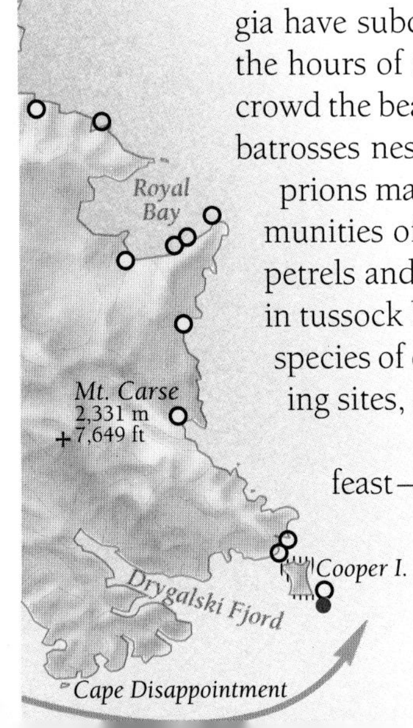

Monument to an era of exploitation, the abandoned whaling town of Grytviken rusts away.

pigments in their eyes enable them to see their prey at great depths. A small colony of Weddell seals at the southern tip of the island favors a diet of fish, while the legions of fur seals eat krill, making shallow dives to feed at night, when krill migrate up to the surface of the sea.

Except for the king penguins, which dive to depths of 700 feet to seize squid and fish, most of South Georgia's penguins survive on krill. On land, penguins may trundle around a bit awkwardly, but underwater they shoot through the sea like torpedoes. Most feed by day, jetting off with powerful flipper strokes at speeds of up to 15 miles an hour to pursue krill as they sink down the water column, away from sun.

The gentoo penguins, sporting trim white headbands, and the macaronis, with their orange punk-plumes, forage in different parts of the sea—the gentoos near shore, the macaronis farther out—in a strategy that not only reduces competition for food but also is tied to the survival of their chicks. Gentoos lay two eggs and rear their young on krill and fish caught inshore. While two chicks might survive in a good season, the gentoos risk total breeding failure in years when krill stocks near the island are poor. The macaronis invest all their energy in raising one chick on a richer diet of pure krill, the parents ranging far offshore where the swarms are more certain to be found. Some biologists estimate that the macaronis alone consume three-fourths of the krill eaten by seabirds around South Georgia; so successful have they been that they form one of the largest concentrations of penguins in the world, with breeding pairs numbering more than five million.

From a distance, you might hear a colony of macaronis before you see them, their collective calls rising and falling in pulses of sound so loud that sailors have navigated the shoreline on foggy days by the noise—and smell—of a familiar rookery. Macaronis nest on steep coasts other penguins won't scale, stippling walls of bare rock in pointillist-dot masses so tightly packed that from the sea the dark slopes themselves seem to waver. During the breeding season, the parents take shifts: One swims out to forage offshore while the other stays at the nest. They trade duties until their chick is big enough to be safe from marauding skuas that patrol the skies with eyes keen for the weak and the injured—or a lapse in parental attention that leaves a youngster open to attack. Each day, the macaronis head out to sea and come home like rush-hour commuters, landing on traditional rocks from which a trail leads uphill through the colony. By late afternoon, freeway-style traffic jams form on the slopes, with penguins backed up in flippering snarls, thinning out as they branch off on exit-ramp

paths to their nests, until the last ones reach the top of the cliffs—for some, a 45-minute trek up from the sea.

Amid the din and density of the colony, parents and chicks recognize each other mainly by voice and perhaps also by individual patterns and coloring. Although different penguin species are best distinguished by facial markings and head plumage, all penguin bodies are countershaded in black and white, a protective coloration that is both a defense and a hunting disguise in the sea. Viewed from above, their black backs blend in with the dark depths beneath them; from below, their white bellies merge with the skylit surface. Their tuxedo tones help penguins steal up on prey—and slip past their mortal enemy, the leopard seal. Cruising the waters off South Georgia, the leopard seal—a sinuous, swift carnivore up to 13 feet long—often lurks near the shores of penguin colonies, waiting for the flocks to plunge in. Sometimes the penguins poise on the rocks ready to dive, hesitant and edgy, stepping forward and back—no one wants to go first. They sense danger, and some say that the penguins' vocal repertoire of honks and brays, trills and wails includes a distinct warning call—an urgent babble that means "leopard seal."

Like the macaronis, most of the other penguins, seals, and seabirds that come to South Georgia breed in synchrony with the boom-and-bust food cycle of the southern ocean. In the waning light of autumn, when photosynthesis slows in the sea, phytoplankton blooms disappear, and the krill populations dependent on them disperse. Most animals rear their young to maturity and depart from the island before winter; among the exceptions is a most remarkable seabird—the magnificant albatross known as the wanderer.

With a wingspread of up to 12 feet, the wandering albatross is the largest seabird in the world. On flat, narrow wings extended like swords, wanderers glide through gales, using the wind's energy so efficiently that they seem to defy the physical limitations of flight. Like ships under sail, they tack back and forth, soaring leeward and down to the surface of the sea, turning windward and gliding up with the momentum of the swoop, until—just before stalling in midair like a barnstormer—they keel over and race back down to the sea. Their endlessly mesmerizing flight has long fascinated sailors, who often watch a lone albatross follow their ship for days on end—without ever flapping a wing.

Wanderers are among the longest-lived birds on earth, perhaps reaching ages of 80 years. Their plumage grows paler over time, and on South Georgia the most ancient wanderers appear snow white. Birds with such long life-spans take years to reach maturity. When a young wandering albatross fledges and leaves South Georgia, it heads out over the southern ocean, where it gradually perfects its flight. Roaming a watery realm ten times the size of the United States, it circles the globe—and may not return to land for seven years.

It is November, and from a tiny islet off the coast of South Georgia a wanderer can be seen in the distance, approaching fast. He arches his wings in a scimitar curve, drops his feet, and stumbles through the tussock grass to a flapping halt. He's an older male, and he's just come home. Albatrosses are monogamous, forming pair bonds for life, and they return to the same nest sites each spring to meet their mates after months of solitary wandering at sea. Males usually fly in first, and immediately this one starts building a nest—a neat, volcano-shaped mound cupped at the top to hold an egg. When his partner arrives a few days later, they court, bowing and caressing and clacking their bills. Then, facing her, the male raises his head to the sky, and with a long, whinnying cry stretches his wings open in full, glorious width, as if to embrace the world and his mate and the wild winds that carried them there.

After the ceremonies of courtship and mating, the female lays an egg, and the wanderers take turns—one feeding at sea while the other incubates the egg. On the nest the birds sit immobile, oblivious to gales and blizzards. They seem to

Fearless in the absence of native land enemies, a group of king penguins eyes a rare tourist.

enter a trance, and often when a foraging wanderer returns to relieve its mate, it must nuzzle and cajole—and physically push its partner off the nest. When the chick hatches ten weeks later, the parents alternately guard and feed at sea. Throughout the incubation and brooding periods, they make incredible journeys over the ocean, traveling at speeds of up to 50 miles an hour and covering distances as great as 9,300 miles in only four weeks. They fly by day and by the light of the moon. At night they settle down on the water to feed on squid and to rest. For the wanderers, the availability of squid in the southern ocean year-round is central to their survival, for they are still bound to South Georgia in winter. Young wanderers cannot fly until nine months after they hatch in March—early autumn in the Southern Hemisphere—and all through the bleak winter months, the chicks remain on their nests.

Young wanderers are fattened with squid, and like penguins and seals, which are protected by a layer of blubber, they are well insulated from the cold. Once the chicks are too large to be harassed by skuas, they have no enemies on land. In contrast to the Arctic, where seabirds and seals face hungry mammals like polar bears and wolves on shore, the creatures that breed in the Antarctic have evolved without any natural terrestrial predators. Every visitor to South

Georgia is struck by the utter fearlessness of the animals toward humans. You can ease up to a nesting albatross, and he'll gaze at you serenely, or stroll near seal pups frolicking inland from the sea. If you crouch near a path used by penguins, they'll stop, look, and cock their heads with curiosity.

South Georgia's wildlife has little to fear from man now, but this was not always so. In a sheltered bay on the east coast of the island stands a cluster of rusting buildings. It is an old settlement called Grytviken, a memorial to an era of exploitation and human greed. It began with the arrival of sailors who came, like the seabirds and seals, to the shores of South Georgia each spring. The first ones were tipped off by Captain Cook. Although he wasted no sympathy on the island, Cook made an observation in his journal that profoundly affected the future of South Georgia. "Seals or Sea Bears were pretty numerous," he wrote, "the Shores swarm'd with young cubs."

Less than 15 years after Cook's discovery, a gold rush for seals began. Vessels from Europe and North America abandoned the depleted rookeries of the Northern Hemisphere and headed south to new hunting grounds. Taking fur seals for skins and elephant seals for oil, they turned South Georgia into a highly profitable killing field. In 1792, 50 tons of elephant seal oil and 50,000 fur seal skins were loaded up in four months—by a single vessel. As early as 1802 the fur seal population on South Georgia had been so seriously reduced that sealing there was no longer economical, and the vessels set sail for other Antarctic isles. Enough seals survived, however, that their numbers slowly recovered, and in the 1800s, there were two more rushes to the island, though primarily for elephant seal oil. By 1886 fur seals had become so scarce that a sealer reported from South Georgia, ". . . we did not get a seal and only saw one."

The greatest slaughter on South Georgia was yet to come. In the early 1900s, whalers arrived, driven south by the overhunting of whales in other oceans. Whales from humpbacks to blues frequented the waters around South Georgia in summer, drawn there by the unusually rich seas. After the founding of a processing station at Grytviken in 1904, South Georgia became the center of the world's whaling industry. The largest whale ever recorded, a female blue more than 110 feet long, was hauled ashore at Grytviken in 1912.

That same year a brig named *Daisy* arrived at South Georgia. It would be the last old-time sealing vessel to come to the island, and along with the crew the ship carried a man named Robert Cushman Murphy, a young American naturalist who came to make collections and observations of the wildlife. His research on South Georgia laid the foundation for a distinguished career in natural history, but his visit also hinted at another era to come. In the early 1900s the British, who govern South Georgia, extended full protection to fur and Weddell seals, and eventually to elephant seals. The 1920s saw the introduction of factory whaling ships, which could catch and process whales on the high seas without needing a land base. Grytviken and other whaling stations on South Georgia slowly declined. By 1965, when the last station closed, not only had whaling ceased to be profitable, but a new sensibility about wildlife and the limits of natural resources had begun to take hold as well—a sensibility fittingly expressed by Robert Cushman Murphy's return to South Georgia in 1970. He arrived this time aboard a natural-history tourist ship and came ashore once again at Grytviken—to meet scientists studying wildlife.

Since the time of Murphy's first visit, elephant seals have rebounded, and fur seals have made an astonishing resurgence, with a population that may near the numbers present when Cook claimed the island two centuries ago. Whales, however, are still seldom seen; they may require decades to recover, and some speculate that the success of the fur seals and of penguins like the macaronis may be linked to the absence of whales feeding on the krill they all need to survive. While protection now exists for much of South Georgia's wildlife, new threats loom. Like ships of earlier times, fishing vessels are leaving the dwindling stocks of northern seas to come south and harvest krill, and great numbers of albatrosses are being lost each year to long lines set for tuna in Southern Hemisphere seas. It is not difficult to imagine the long-term effect of krill harvests, or of the loss of birds that take so long to mature, or of the impact of human actions on the high seas—so far from the eyes of the world—on a small island in the southern ocean that once again holds the wondrous array of life it had before the world knew it was there.

By June, when the Antarctic winter sets in, South Georgia is nearly deserted. Gales howl through the mountains; snows pack the valleys; the days pass like twilight. Most of the seals and seabirds have long since dispersed to the southern ocean, but in a field of tussock a wandering albatross chick waits. It's downy and plump now and the size of an adult, but it still cannot fly. Until recently many believed that wanderer chicks were abandoned in the dreadful winter months, that they survived on reserves of fat, seated on their nests, alone. But actually the chicks are still fed by their parents, which must range over thousands of square miles of open ocean wilderness, riding the black gales of winter, to forage for the squid that sustains them and their young.

All through those months of darkness and blizzards, the albatross chick must practice patience. But underneath its downy coat, feathers are growing, and by the time the sun rises high in the sky and the seals return to the beaches, roaring, the young wanderer has become a true bird. One day in late spring it steps down from its nest, a bit wobbly still. It flaps, stumbles, and stretches its wings, and then, facing the wild ocean wind, it runs forward, lifts up, and flies.

F*rom a promontory, I watched* Damien II *(opposite) get pummeled by a shrieking gale.* This *yacht carried me on an extraordinary voyage around* South Georgia. *For nearly three months we did not see another vessel, but we had frequent encounters with elephant seals (above) emerging from tussock grass and made landfalls near enormous penguin colonies, such as this gathering of kings (following pages) in* St. Andrews Bay.

Stretching out flippers and feet to soak up the sun on a rare balmy day, a downy gentoo chick (below) snoozes while its parents forage offshore. Returning in late afternoon with a crop of krill and tiny fish, a parent (opposite) is ready to regurgitate food for its offspring, which will be reared to independence during the brief Antarctic summer.

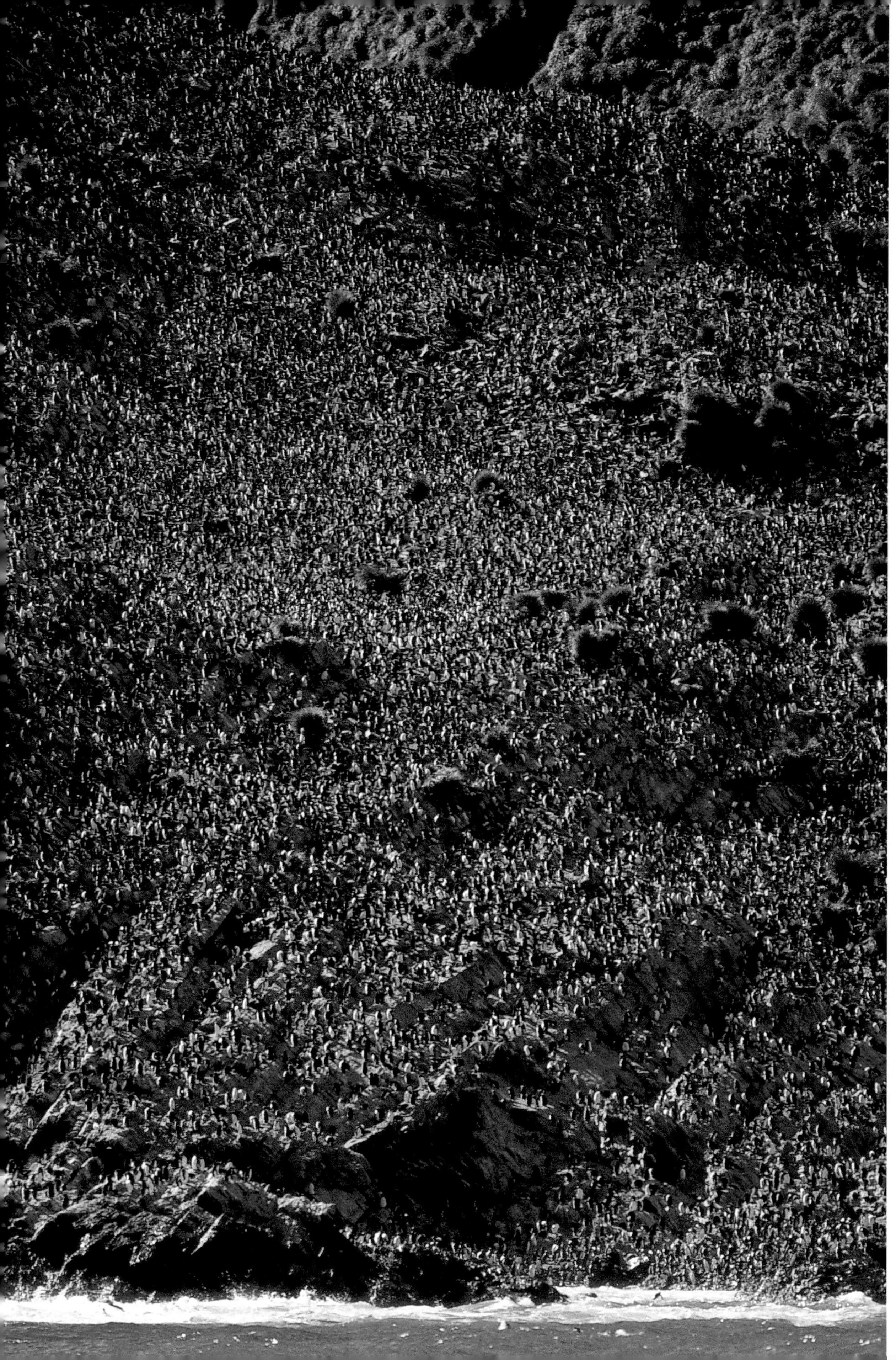

Impressed by their gusto, I documented how a raft of macaronis (below) leaped ashore from a crashing wave at the base of a crowded colony (opposite). I was amazed to discover traditional trails leading uphill through the colony, where the rocks had been worn smooth over the ages by the passing of millions of clawed penguin feet.

A bitter wind blows through the bowels of deserted Leith Harbour (*below*), *a whaling town that still smells of stale whale* 25 *years after the last one was killed.* Outside, *in a whalers' cemetery* (*opposite*), *old sorrow mixes with new life. Against a background of crosses that testifies to the harsh lives of young men who died far from home, an* Antarctic *tern has laid a fresh egg—to me a fragile symbol of a new era of conservation.*

With shock, I recognized the ripple effect of the great whales' demise. Their ecological niche has been filled in part by fur seals, also krill eaters, whose numbers have risen to such a height that they are now denuding the land around their colonies (above). With newborn innocence, a baby fur seal (opposite), in a rare blond color phase, strikes a sinuous mermaid pose for me as I wade around in the icy water.

At dusk, South Georgia comes alive with the whirl of wings as millions of petrels return to land from feeding offshore; others come out of underground burrows, where they tend their eggs and young. Relatively safe from the marauding skuas, which rule the skies by day, a pair of white-chinned petrels (below) exchange chittering courtship calls under the protective cover of darkness.

Combining the rapacious qualities of gull and hawk, a skua attacks a

young albatross that has come too close to the skua's nest.

One evening near the end of my voyage, I *watched how* South Georgia *faded into midnight twilight, and* I *realized* I *had come to know this island at the end of the earth as an* Eden *on which millions of wild lives depend.* Even *the wanderer (above), that glorious nomad—known to soar the southern ocean for years at a time on outstretched wings without ever touching solid ground—needs this outpost of land in a freezing sea to perpetuate its kind.*

HAWAII
The Farthest Paradise

W*atching the sun set over* Maui*, it's easy to be lulled by the soft charm of* Hawaii. *To many, the very name of these islands evokes images of harmony and a world totally benign. Yet here I witnessed nature in the raw as it shapes the land by fire and water in a never ending process of creation and destruction. From the rim of* Pu'u 'O'o *on the island of* Hawaii *(overleaf), you look into the heart of the earth, from which lava pulses outward in fiery geysers. Born of fire like all the islands,* Kauai's Na Pali *coast shows the subsequent weathering by water on a monumental scale (following pages).*

Cracks in a cooled lava flow provide footholds for shoots of the ʻamaʻu *fern.*

The First to Arrive

Gray clouds roll up the mountain and billow over the summit like smoke. They mass around the peak, gathering and swelling as if the mountain were spinning them into a storm. Far below, the setting sun still shines on the lowland forests, but as light drains from the sky and darkness comes, the clouds above the mountain still glow. They flush soft crimson with another light, reflected from the hot heart of the earth. The mountain is an active volcano, a seething caldron of wild orange lava. Inside, a fiery lake roils and bubbles. Great domes of liquid rock balloon up and explode in ragged red starbursts, splattering the black crater walls like fireworks against a night sky. Bright veins of lava course between slabs of dark crust on the surface that crack apart like shifting continental plates. Underneath, the lava moves like a tide in the sea. From the rim it sounds as if the ocean is roaring inside, breakers booming and hissing and building to crash. Heat rises and presses over the rim like hot breath, and as heavy rains pelt down and hard gusts blow, the volcano churns on—a force greater than anything the world above can hurl at the molten rock boiled up from deep in the earth.

Many times the volcano has shot fountains of lava high into the sky or spilled flaming flows down its slopes, and daylight reveals their paths. The flanks of the cone are stained with twining black braids, broad black rivers, and fanning black deltas of lava. It looks as lifeless as the moon, but not far from the rim of the crater, on a stream of chunky lava just a few months old, a green fern shivers in the wind. Not long after the lava cooled, a fern spore drifted in. It lodged in a crevice where enough moisture collected, and it grew, uncurling a small fiddlehead that opened into a tiny red frond, poking up like a lick of hot lava. Then it rose a bit higher, spread its palm to the sun, and greened as if in sheer defiance of the naked rock where it took root.

The place where the fern grows is a huge volcanic cone known as Pu'u 'O'o. Since 1983, Pu'u 'O'o has rumbled and exploded and surged to a height of 835 feet on the slope of an even bigger mountain, Kilauea—one of the most active volcanoes on earth. Together they rise on the island of Hawaii, the largest and southernmost of the Hawaiian Islands. From Hawaii—often called the Big Island to distinguish it from the group as a whole—the other isles stretch northwest in a chain for 1,500 miles across the middle of the Pacific Ocean. They are the most remote island group in the world. Although the reach of the Hawaiian Islands is

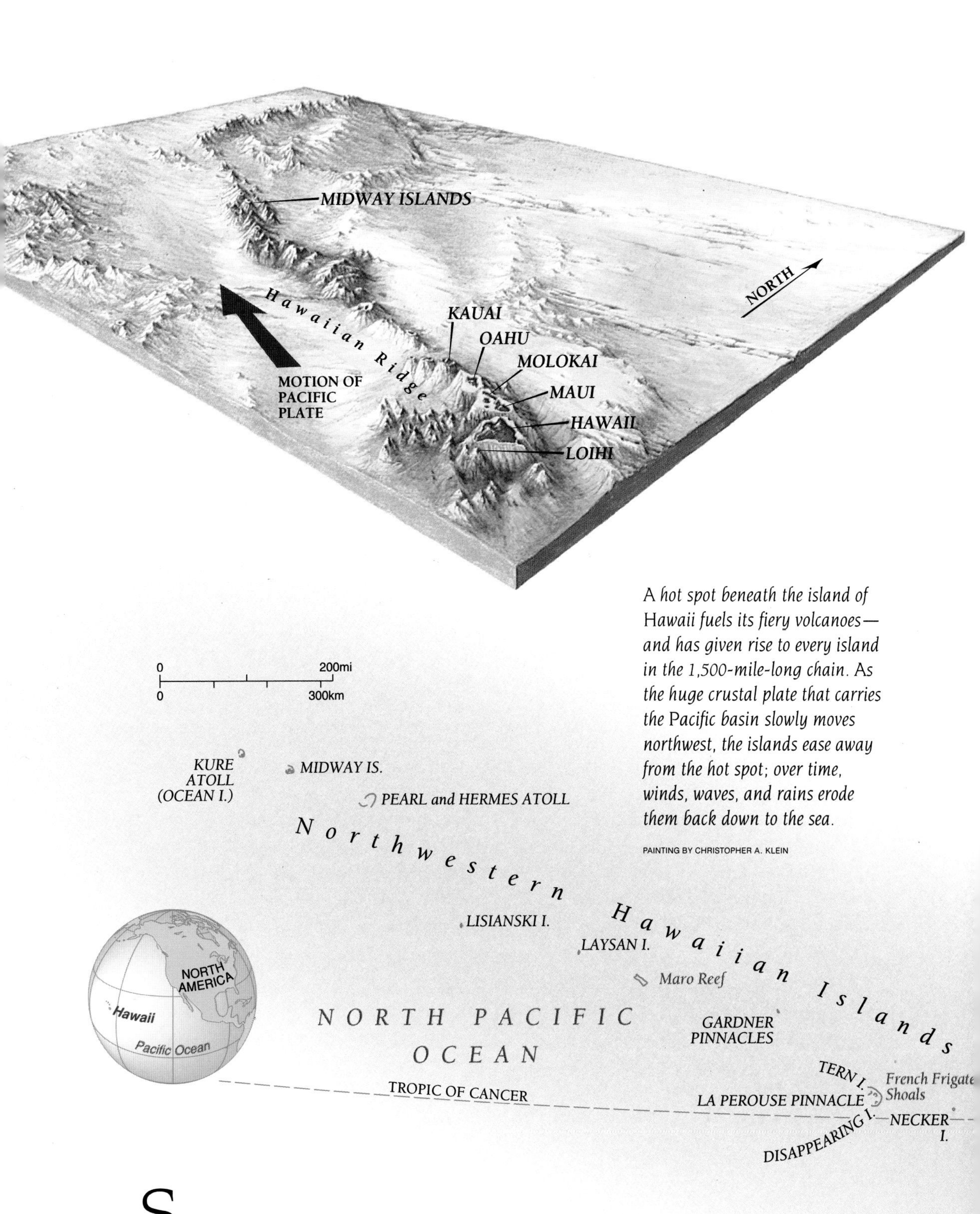

A hot spot beneath the island of Hawaii fuels its fiery volcanoes—and has given rise to every island in the 1,500-mile-long chain. As the huge crustal plate that carries the Pacific basin slowly moves northwest, the islands ease away from the hot spot; over time, winds, waves, and rains erode them back down to the sea.

PAINTING BY CHRISTOPHER A. KLEIN

Sprinkled in a line across the central Pacific, the Hawaiian Islands make up the most remote island group in the world. Built by volcanoes, all were colonized by plants and animals from distant lands—accidental arrivals that drifted across sea or sky to the shores of Hawaii.

long, they have never been attached to a continent. They arose from the bottom of the sea. All were built by volcanoes like the bubbling new cone on Kilauea; and all were first colonized by pioneers like the tiny fern, blown in from lands thousands of miles away. The power of the volcano and the miracle of the fern are the story of life on Hawaii.

There are more than a hundred Hawaiian Islands, and geography divides the group in two. The eight islands that form the southeastern half of the chain—Hawaii, Maui, Kahoolawe, Lanai, Molokai, Oahu, Niihau, and Kauai—contain 99.9 percent of the land. Most are high and mountainous; their lush windward slopes weep with waterfalls. The 90-odd northwestern islands, the Leewards, comprise a total land area of only five square miles. They are rock pinnacles and sandy atolls, low and dry and nearly lost in the sea. Despite the variety in their sizes and forms, and the distances between them now, every Hawaiian island emerged from exactly the same place—and it lies beneath the bubbling cone.

Under the Pacific Ocean, miles below the ocean floor, stirs a layer of fluid rock—the upper mantle of the earth. The continents and seafloors that form earth's outer crust are cracked into puzzle-piece plates that ride atop the mantle like rafts. The Pacific plate, which carries the Hawaiian Islands and most of the huge Pacific Ocean floor, has a small break in its crust known as a hot spot. For tens of millions of years, a plume of liquid rock from the mantle has gushed through the break. It spills onto the ocean floor in thick, viscous pillows and slowly heaps up. For a million years a silent volcano rises, 16,000 feet up from the bottom of the sea, until it bursts through the waves with explosions of lava and geysers of steam, the sizzling tip of a newborn island.

The volcano doesn't stop. Over many ages the island grows higher, perhaps reaching a height great enough that, even in the tropics, winter snows fall on the summit. The island may be so tall—as the Big Island is now—that if measured from the seafloor to the summit, it would exceed the 29,000-foot peak of Mount Everest. Slowly the Pacific plate moves northwest as it has been doing for some 70 million years, and the island is carried away from the hot spot. In its place far down on the ocean floor, a new volcano begins to build.

Each Hawaiian island was formed in this way, arising from the hot spot and then easing northwest, the flaming torch of volcanism passing from isle to isle.

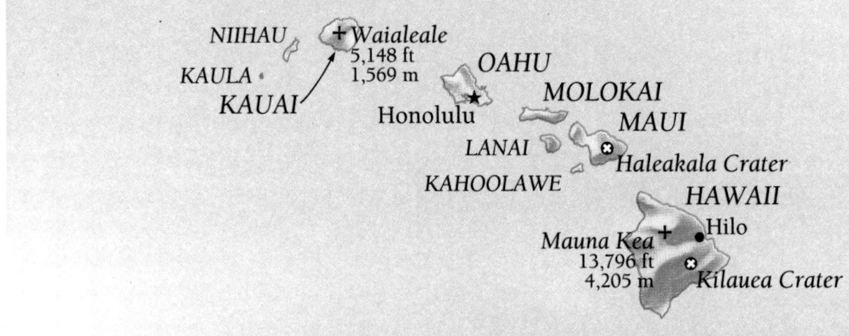

Livestock interests have eradicated the native forests that once covered the slopes of Mauna Kea.

Taken together, the entire Hawaiian chain is an island time line—and a measure of time itself. The Big Island, the colossus and the youngest, is less than a million years old and still growing. The fires that built Kauai, seven islands away, dimmed and died about four million years ago; its heights have eroded and furrowed with time. The outermost Hawaiian island of Kure, 1,200 miles northwest of Kauai, may have stood tall 25 million years ago, but the weathering power of the rains and the wind and the sea has ground it down, leaving only a small ring of coral and sand.

The Hawaiian Islands are perhaps at their loveliest in middle age. Isles like Kauai and Oahu, Molokai and Maui, face the moist northeasterly trade winds, with steep mountains velvet with flowering shrubs and high valleys thick with rain forests. From the sea, their peaks tower up to the clouds in green spires, presenting what Western imagination has come to regard as a picture of paradise. The mountains catch passing clouds and so steadily wring them of rain that

some places are bathed in almost perpetual showers. Kauai's highest peak, Waialeale, is the wettest spot on earth: More than 40 feet of rain falls there each year. Just as the fires from below built the islands to great heights, the rains from above carve their slopes into fantastic flutes and arrowheads, and slowly whittle them back down to the sea. Waialeale is the mountain that built Kauai, but the old black volcano is emerald now, dripping with mosses and ferns, and on the sheer crater walls where red lava once sprayed high into the sky, silver waterfalls tumble down in bridal veils of mist.

When the first Hawaiian island emerged, it stood alone, naked to the sun. No flowers bloomed on its shores; no living thing roamed the land. Most oceanic islands are colonized by flora and fauna from nearby continents, but the Hawaiian Islands lie near the center of the sea that covers one-third of the earth. So vast is the oceanic space surrounding them that the nearest continent is 2,500 miles away. Before the first Polynesians arrived 1,500 years ago, the only plants and animals on Hawaii were those that had survived astonishing passages from distant lands. Some floated across the sea; some drifted through the air; others clung to the bodies of migrating birds. The odds against a species becoming established in Hawaii are enormous: Scientists estimate that in the history of the islands' existence, a successful colonist arrived once every 100,000 years. The tiny fern below the rim of the bubbling cone is one that survived the crossing, and the wonder of its appearance on the lava flow is only surpassed by the journey that carried it there.

There are trails in the seas and skies of the Pacific. Prevailing winds and currents sweep the ocean, providing travel corridors for unwitting castaways: an airborne seed, a floating mat of vegetation, a lost land bird. But the ocean currents that circle the North Pacific basin form a great gyre that bypasses Hawaii, and the three currents that surge eastward and westward across the tropic zone prevent most oceanic drifters from crossing the Equator. A buoyant seed that fell into the sea in the Philippines and strayed by freak chance to Hawaii would have had to withstand months of saltwater soaking and still remain viable when it finally washed ashore. Even so, it is believed that as much as 20 percent of Hawaii's original vegetation reached the islands by sea. Many were coastal strand species like pink beach morning glories and white-flowered *Scaevola* bushes, hardy plants that are found throughout the Indo-Pacific tropics. Others, like the majestic koa tree of Hawaii, probably drifted up 5,000 miles from Australia, where the koa's nearest relative, an acacia, occurs. But its seeds are so heavy they sink in seawater, and scientists speculate that the koa may have come to Hawaii on the rarest of chances—as a branch full of seed pods that swept ashore only once.

By air the odds are even slimmer. For most of the year, northeast trade winds cool the islands, but during the winter months, strong gales from the south blow in. Known as *kona* storms, from the Hawaiian word for "south," they have the power to carry drifting seeds over great distances, but the possibility of success is so remote that scientists consider that less than 2 percent of Hawaii's plants arrived on the wind. However, a remarkable experiment conducted in recent years demonstrated what the winds did bring. Out at sea and far from the islands, scientists stretched nets from ships and planes, and captured a vast array of unexpected atmospheric drifters. They were insects and spiders—small enough to be nearly invisible in the air, light enough to be lofted for thousands of miles. The research showed that Hawaii's insects and spiders could have floated in on the wind—and more: Most of the species netted belonged to the same families now native to the islands.

Hawaii has no native reptiles and amphibians, and its only native mammal is a bat; but the islands have a rich assemblage of tiny land snails, no bigger than a fingertip and colorful with spiraling stripes. Though they seem unlikely candidates for long-distance travel, the snails, as well as three-fourths of the islands' flora, came on other Pacific trails—sky paths printed in the instincts of birds, which carried them all to Hawaii.

Seabirds, shorebirds, and waterfowl range the big skies of the Pacific. Shorebirds like the golden plover and bristle-thighed curlew travel each year from their Arctic breeding grounds south to tropical Oceania and back again; waterfowl routes hug the borders of Asia and the Americas, while seabirds disperse from island nesting sites all across the Pacific. If you looked closely at the white wings of a tropicbird or at a bit of soil caked on the foot of a wandering tattler, you might find a few small seeds. A tiny snail from a mudflat in North America might stick to the breast plumage of a ruddy turnstone; the last meal a golden plover enjoyed before flying south from Alaska in August may have been a feast of ripe berries. A Canada goose tossed far off course by a storm might arrive by good luck in Hawaii—and preen off the grass seeds snagged in its feathers. By such rare flights of fortune did Hawaii's accidental colonists find a first foothold on the black volcanoes.

What of the young green fern? Its passage is perhaps the most remarkable of all. There's yet another path in the Pacific skies. Thirty-five thousand feet up, the jet stream swoops in a great curve from Southeast Asia across the belly of the Pacific. Its winds exceed 120 miles an hour as they leave the Asian continent but slow to nearly half that speed above Hawaii. The spores by which ferns propagate are minuscule—as many as 125 lined up side by side would equal one inch—and they are easily lofted by the wind. Although travel by jet stream from Southeast Asia to Hawaii would take only about two days, the air temperatures are freezing. The fern spores, as fragile as they may seem, survive. If they fall out from the slowing jet stream and drift down to Hawaii, they can thaw and sprout. Most of Hawaii's ferns are descendants of species from Southeast Asia, and they have spread throughout the islands—living proof of their improbable journey.

A Hawaiian island was like an empty planet to the first arrivals, and early on there must have been terrible failures—a seed that landed in the wrong place to grow; a flower that bloomed but lacked a pollinator; a lone bird that arrived but never found a mate. For others, Hawaii was a paradise of possibilities, and they took to the land with vigor. Over time, plants and animals adapted and changed to fit into island environments that range from tropical lowlands to alpine peaks. In the process, they were transformed into something entirely new: life unique to Hawaii. When the first Polynesians stepped ashore, they gazed at a land like no other: Ninety-five percent of Hawaii's flora and fauna could be found nowhere else in the world.

Sometime in the past six million years, a seed from California made its way to Hawaii. It was a tarweed, a member of the huge plant family that includes dandelions, daisies, and sunflowers. When it reached the islands, it flourished with wild abandon. The tarweed moved into every Hawaiian environment except the coastal strand and evolved into a vast array of new forms, from low-lying shrubs to trees 25 feet tall. As such, it is perhaps the premier example of adaptive radiation in the whole of the plant kingdom. The humble tarweed's Hawaiian descendants now include about 30 endemic species known as the silversword alliance—named for one of the most magnificent plants in all Hawaii.

The summit of Maui's highest mountain, Haleakala, is the castle keep of the silversword. It grows on the upper slopes and inside the huge crater of Haleakala, a 10,000-foot-high volcano that last erupted around 1790. The crater itself is more than seven miles wide, and within rise a dozen old volcanic cones, colored in the burnt shades of a painted desert. The soil is red and gold with iron and sulfur, and the winds whirl dusty storms inside. In the rich light of late afternoon, Haleakala glows so vermilion that it resembles a landscape from Mars. The climate is sunbeaten and cold; little life survives in these harsh heights. But scattered through the crater and around the rocky rim lives the silversword. From a distance it looks like a giant pearl nestled among the dark rocks. Up close, you can see that it is a dense rosette of narrow leaves, stiff and upcurved like spears. If you run your fingers along them, they feel as smooth as satin; in moonlight the silverswords glow like fallen stars. Their texture and color is an adaptation to the rarefied air of Haleakala: Each spear is covered with a nap of silvery hairs that deflect the sun and the wind. As lovely as they appear on the bleak summit of Haleakala, the silverswords, once in their lives, do something even more beautiful.

A *museum selection shows the diversity of* Oahu's *land snails, many now extinct.*

When a plant is about 10 or 15 years old, it sends up a stalk six feet tall and then bursts into glorious bloom with hundreds of magenta blossoms—the silversword's grand effort to seed, after which it withers and dies.

A few thousand feet down from the summit, Haleakala's rocky slopes yield to a shrubland forest of yellow-flowered mamani trees, sweet-scented sandalwood, and groves of gnarled *'ohi'as* thick with red, brushy bouquets. If you wait long enough, you might notice small flashes of red and yellow zipping overhead like flickers of fire and sun in the trees. If you're lucky, you might see the tiny birds feed—a golden *'amakihi* sipping mamani nectar; a scarlet *'i'iwi* dipping in to taste the 'ohi'a's ambrosia, its long decurved bill held high as it perches, giving the diminutive 'i'iwi a very brave countenance.

The little birds are honeycreepers, a unique family of Hawaiian land birds that originated from a single colonization—perhaps a group of finches from the Americas, swept out by a powerful storm. Land birds are among the rarest of Hawaiian immigrants, and from a mere 15 arrivals over many millions of years, more than a hundred endemic species arose. Most of them are members of the honeycreeper tribe, and some of them evolved bill in blossom with Hawaii's flora. A family portrait of the honeycreepers sketched in profile reveals an amazing variety of bills—from hooked and stubby ones to slender needlelike ones, arced like scythes. The bill of the *'akiapola'au,* affectionately nicknamed "the Swiss-army-knife bird," has a bit of both features—a stout lower mandible used to peck at tree bark and a long curved upper one to pry out insect larvae. Other honeycreepers developed their unusual bills to extract the nectar from a certain family of plants, the lobelias. Hawaii's lobelias probably came from the Andes, and like the honeycreepers they changed into a great number of new forms. Among them are lobelias with long decurved blossoms that precisely match the shapes of the honeycreepers' bills. The birds and the flowers coevolved in Hawaii, the birds' bills growing longer as the blossoms grew deeper. With its specialized bill, a honeycreeper could feed exclusively on a certain lobelia, and as it reached in to drink from bloom to bloom, it became the plant's sole pollinator.

In its supreme isolation, life in Hawaii took some unusual twists and turns. In the absence of reptiles and amphibians, Nihoa's *Banza* grasshopper could eat the larger foods they might have consumed, and over time it became a giant. In forests with a limited assortment of trees, some normally small plants grew leggy and arborescent like the eight-foot-tall violet of Kauai's rain forest. Without their continental predators, some crickets, beetles—and even birds—lost the need to fly; Hawaiian plants no longer developed poisons, thorns, or odors to deter the

munch of mammals. The seeds of many plants grew larger and heavier as it became advantageous for their seedlings to take root in what was already an ideal spot, rather than be carried away. Ironically, many species lost the ability to disperse that had originally brought them to the islands. By 1,500 years ago, Hawaii had become a lush but vulnerable Eden—and then the Polynesians arrived.

Like the ancestors of Hawaii's flora and fauna, the Polynesians made unparalleled oceanic passages. Beginning in island Asia around 2500 B.C., they fanned out eastward and in three thousand years' time colonized the isles of the Pacific—from New Zealand across to Easter Island and north to Hawaii. They traveled in outrigger canoes, navigating by winds and currents, stars and birds, with skills unsurpassed by any other people on earth. They read patterns in waves deflected from distant isles to detect that land lay beyond the horizon. They followed birds at sea to home in on an unseen island, knowing the range that each species ventured from shore. As widely spread as the Pacific isles are, most of them are separated by little more than 200 miles. The first Polynesians to reach Hawaii came from the Marquesas, 2,500 miles to the southeast. To make such a crossing required a great leap of faith, and we may never know what impelled the journey. One charming notion suggests that golden plovers may have provided an inspiration: Those that overwinter in southern Pacific isles like the Marquesas often stop in Hawaii each spring on their way north to the Arctic, and perhaps the ancient voyagers followed the birds.

The Polynesians were colonists and brought animals and food plants with them to establish settlements in a new land. Hawaii had never felt the footprint of a mammal, and its life was helpless in the face of creatures like pigs, rats, dogs, and human hunters. The islands once held a unique megafauna that included a giant flightless goose and ibis, a crow the size of a raven, and even a huge honeycreeper; but they were among the first to vanish. As the Polynesians cleared coastal plains and valleys for crops, much of the islands' lowland forests disappeared, and with them species we will never know. By the late 18th century, the main islands were densely populated, although the highly ordered Hawaiian society had achieved a certain balance with the land. Then the Europeans arrived.

The pace of change accelerated exponentially. Forests were cleared for timber, ranches, and plantations; more animals were introduced: cattle, goats, sheep, and other livestock; cats, birds, and other pets. Feral animals roamed the land, as they continue to do today. Pigs rooted through native bogs and forests, and grew especially fond of native orchids and tree ferns; dogs preyed upon seabirds and the only surviving Hawaiian goose, the nene; goats ate the silverswords of Haleakala. Even lowlier introductions have taken a horrific toll: Carnivorous snails devoured most of the native land snails; and ants, which had never reached the islands on their own, now consume many of Hawaii's native caterpillars—as well as the bees and moths that pollinate the silverswords. Since the early 1800s, when mosquitoes accidentally arrived on a ship from Mexico, most of the honeycreepers living below 3,000 feet have succumbed to avian malaria, against which they have no natural defense. To date, more species of plants and animals have forever disappeared from Hawaii than from all of North America.

The Hawaiian landscape is still luscious and dreamy, but much of its beauty is pantropical, derived from exotics brought in from all over the world—bougainvilleas from South America, oleanders from Asia Minor, frangipanis from tropic America, flamboyants from Madagascar. On the road that snakes up Haleakala, you may pass jacarandas from Brazil, gardens of South African proteas, eucalypts from Australia, and North American pines, before you reach the rocky cloudland of the silverswords. Even the birdsong of Hawaii rings with the strange notes of Indian mynahs, Japanese white eyes, and American cardinals. Native Hawaiian environments survive as islands within the islands—volcanic peaks and plunging cliff faces; a mountaintop swamp on Kauai; an unapproachable headland on Molokai; patches of forest on the Big Island known as *kipukas,* which are completely surrounded by lava flows; the exquisite but inaccessible hanging valleys on Kauai's Na Pali coast. Given the fragility of Hawaiian life, it is miraculous that even this much remains, but only given the most drastic of protective measures will it hold out.

Parks and reserves shelter a number of native habitats now, and more are needed. At sites like Kilauea Point, a wildlife refuge on the north coast of Kauai, a high fence has been erected to prevent four-legged animals from entering. Beyond the chain links whirls a snowstorm of seabirds. Most are red-footed boobies that nest along the steep cliffs, but among them soar elegant Laysan albatrosses, ground-nesting birds whose eggs and chicks fall prey to dogs and feral animals. Now these birds are increasing in number, as are the ground-nesting shearwaters atop the cliffs, whose eerie wails from their underground burrows at dusk join the wild, high cries of the boobies and the giddy courtship song of the albatrosses in a music that sounds like renewal.

Though it roams the North Pacific, the Laysan albatross is a Hawaiian native too, but its nesting stronghold is in the Leeward Islands northwest of Kauai, most of which are protected as a wildlife refuge. Islands like Nihoa, the closest to Kauai, are rocky chips of old volcanic craters, while older isles like the French Frigate Shoals are rings of white sandy atolls set in turquoise shallows—the sparkling afterglow of where a volcano once rose; farther northwest, the Pearl and Hermes Reef looks as insubstantial as cirrus clouds that fell from the sky.

Although many of the Leewards are barely visible from the sea, millions of animals know exactly where they are. More than six million seabirds raise their young on the islets and atolls, and up from the sea to nest and bask on the beaches come thousands of rare green sea turtles and the last of the Hawaiian monk seals, one of the most endangered animals in the world. For the seabirds and turtles, the Leewards are a critical habitat; for the seals, they are a final sanctuary. The animals crowd the tiny slivers of sand—monk seals with their pups, turtles resting in the sun—while pillars of seabirds swirl overhead: albatrosses, frigatebirds, and boobies; tropicbirds, terns, and shearwaters. All are creatures of the sea, but they rely for a crucial moment in their lives upon the faraway strand of isles sprinkled across the middle of the Pacific.

Beneath the waves that wash the islands, the turtles and seals feed on the flanks of ancient volcanoes—islands that loomed high and smoldered with fire when the monk seal migrated to Hawaiian waters from the Caribbean about 15 million years ago. The sea turtle, whose lineage dates back perhaps 200 million years, probably scratched a nest on the beach of the first Hawaiian island; the seabirds, whose ancestry is nearly half as old as the turtles', may have alighted on the new land and shaken seeds from their wings.

In the long view of geologic time, the Hawaiian Islands themselves are a fiery wink. They rise up from the sea and melt back into the waves as another emerges anew, speaking fables of impermanence and eternity. Under the seas off the Big Island, not far from Kilauea and the flames of Pu'u 'O'o, a volcano named Loihi is quietly building. It is already 13,000 feet tall—but still 3,000 feet below the surface of the sea. It will take 10,000 years or more, but when Loihi explodes through the waves and cools enough to collect a bit of rain, perhaps a fern will be the first to raise its head to the sun.

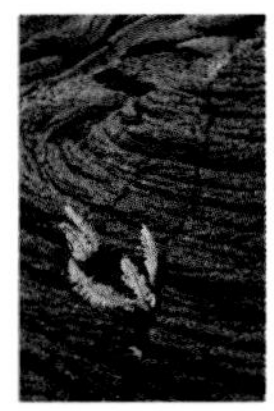

Though mere miles from beaches visited by millions, the jungle interiors of the Hawaiian Islands *are a world apart.* Places *like the cloud forest of* Kamakou *near the summit of* Molokai *(following pages) represent the hidden heart of an older, wilder* Hawaii. *In the mysterious boggy realm of* Kauai's Alakai Swamp, *where sundews glisten (above) and near-extinct birds flitter, I barely covered a mile a day, struggling through luxuriant undergrowth.* Nearby, *waterfalls plunge* 2,000 *feet down the crater walls of* Waialeale, *considered the wettest spot on earth.*

From a new vent at the base of Pu'u 'O'o, *itself but a recent outgrowth of the giant volcano* Kilauea, *lava gushes out and engulfs the last vestiges of the forest that once grew there.* From the air, *the landscape looks devastated; it is an awesome display of the earth's utter indifference to its own makings.* But *just downslope, I'm reminded of the philosopher who wrote,* "Nature *abhors a vacuum.*" There, *on a lava field only a few years old, in sight of the still-spewing volcano,* 'ama'u *ferns and* 'ohi'a *trees are taking root—the vanguard of a future forest.*

To see Hawaii *as the first* Polynesians *found it,* I *had to go to the edge.* Only *in isolated habitats do remnants of the archipelago's original flora survive.* Huelo Rock *(left), a sea stack off* Molokai, *is a last stronghold for the native palm called* loulu. A Hawaiian *friend told me that a long time ago, young men would climb the cliffs and jump into the ocean using large fan-shaped loulu leaves as parachutes.* In *the rarefied atmosphere of* Mauna Kea's *upper slopes,* I *encountered another survivor.* How *silverswords (opposite) manage to thrive in a near-lifeless lunar landscape at* 11,000 *feet is as miraculous to me as the story of their ancestry:* They *descend from a simple* American*-daisy relative, carried to the islands as seeds snagged in the plumage of a bird blown off course.*

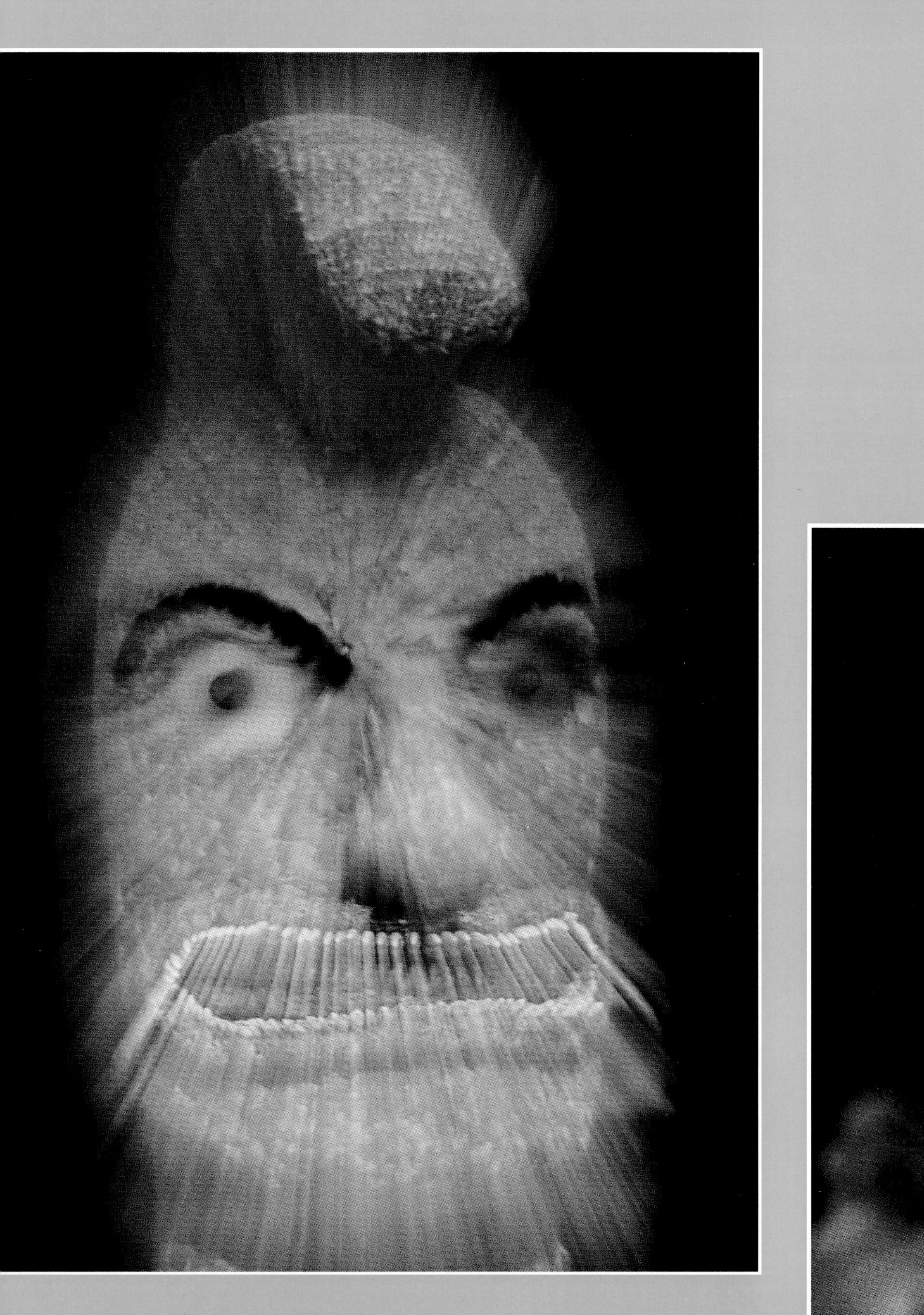

Hawaii's honeycreepers are one of the world's most remarkable examples of island evolution. More than a hundred *kinds are believed to have evolved from a single species that reached the islands by chance.* But *few of these have been able to withstand the onslaught of later invaders.* Early Hawaiians *collected them by the thousand for feathered cloaks and helmets, such as this one staring with shell eyes from a museum display.* Even *more catastrophic to* Hawaii's *birds has been the accidental introduction of mosquitoes, which transmit avian malaria.* Today, *forests at lower elevations are eerily silent; only higher up can one catch glimpses of native wonders like the* ʻiʻiwi (*below*).

Ground down by the forces of weather and time, Midway's Eastern Island (above) was once part of a mighty volcano like those far to the southeast; now it's a mere pancake of coral rubble a few feet above sea level. But in its dying days as an island, it serves as an essential cradle and nursery to marine wildlife. Offshore, green turtles (opposite) float lazily in tranquil lagoons. Onshore, the nesting colonies of many thousands of sooty terns are marked by a swirl of birds and an incessant din (preceding pages).

Whale-Skate Island in the French Frigate Shoals is a remote speck of land inhabited by blue-faced boobies nesting on the beach and monk seals flipping sand on their heads in a futile attempt to create shade. One memorable day I wandered among them, reveling in the fact that they barely took notice of me and realizing that my brief intrusion on their privacy would not be more than a ripple in their wild lives.

MADAGASCAR
Gondwana's Ark

Perched on a platform high above the forest floor, I exchanged glances with a bug-eyed lepilemur, one of many extraordinary faces in the forests of Madagascar. On *this fabled island, I witnessed chameleons strike with pinpoint accuracy (overleaf).* And I *wandered through woodlands full of life-forms that evolved in splendid isolation, such as these orchids (following pages) cascading over a stream in the eastern rain forest.*

A *tribesman holds the egg of* Aepyornis maximus, *the world's largest bird, extinct since the 1600s.*

Nowhere in the World But Here

First light from the east reaches over the land, outlining a dark plain with strange forms: a tree that seems to stand with its roots to the sky; another that resembles a swollen candelabra; groves of straight spiked boughs 30 feet high, clumped like sheaves of thorned snakes. Beyond them rise shaggy pillars crowned with speared rosettes and tall mazes of cactuslike trees whose forked arms trace wild zigzags against the dawn sky, like black lightning sparked up from the earth.

The sun eases higher, finding moisture and whiteness in the shadows. It sparkles the dew on a spider web and brightens the angel-white fur of a beautiful animal edging up a spiked bough to the halo of light at the top. The animal looks like a monkey with a long tail that curls and switches as it creeps higher, exhaling puffs of gold breath against the rising sun. Its face suggests a young fox and is black, with huge topaz eyes that gleam like lighted windows in the night. Its fur is silky and ermine and still twinkles with condensation as it reaches a warm patch of light. Bending down, it licks the moisture from its chest and shoulders, then raises both arms as if to bow to the dawn, closes its eyes, and sunbathes.

Three more of the animals appear, grunting softly to one another as they scale up to the sunlight. They are sifakas, a species of lemur—primates like ourselves—and their name is onomatopoeic for the sound of their alarm call: *Shee-faak!* they cry, when danger is near. Like almost every plant in the spiny desert forests that stretch for many miles around them, the sifakas live nowhere in the world but here, on the Indian Ocean island of Madagascar.

Beneath the boughs where the sifakas rest runs a small sandy creek. The summer rains that sometimes fail to come to this land have been good this year. Heavy torrents swelled the dry veins of the desert, rushing into wide brown rivers that flow down to the sea. The rains have ended, and the creek below the sifakas is dry again now; but the sudden surge of water has scoured away several inches of sand, revealing a pale mound, still half-buried. It glows creamy white in the morning sun, and catches the eye of a man passing near. He has walked this land every day of his life, tending his cattle, and when he sees the mound, he knows exactly what it is. The sifakas bound off through the boughs, calling their names, then stop and watch from a distance as the man scoops away sand and lifts up a great white globe, cradling it with care, as though he held a small moon just fallen from the sky.

A *hillside bristles with the outlandish vegetation of southern Madagascar's spiny desert.*

It is an egg, and it belongs to the largest bird that ever walked the earth, *Aepyornis maximus*—the elephant bird. Resembling a gigantic ostrich, it stood almost ten feet tall and weighed about a thousand pounds. Its name dates back to an account by the 13th-century traveler Marco Polo, who recorded tales from Arab traders of a bird in Madagascar so huge that it could "pounce on an elephant and carry it up to a great height in the air." The Arabs called it *roc,* the giant bird fabled in *The Thousand and One Nights* that lifted Sindbad the Sailor from a faraway island up to the heavens and down to a valley sprinkled with diamonds.

Though *Aepyornis maximus* was flightless, it was real, and its amazing size surely inspired the tales of the roc. Now extinct, the big bird still lived in Marco Polo's time, and to this day its eggs emerge from the land, some with fossil embryos inside. They are relics of a past age and a perfect symbol for Madagascar. Beyond the spiny desert stretch plains of dry forests, pinnacled limestone plateaus, rolling highland savannas, and mountains draped with rain forests down to the sea. All are full of plants and animals whose ancestral forms once lived on other continents. That was millions of years ago. Today many survive—in forms both little changed and new—only in Madagascar, an island that is, like

the ancient eggs still buried in its sands, a time capsule of another era on earth.

Madagascar lies in the southwest Indian Ocean, 250 miles east of Mozambique, moored like a smaller vessel near the mother ship of Africa. Nearly 1,000 miles long and 360 miles wide, it is the fourth largest island in the world—though once Madagascar was landlocked. About 180 million years ago, Africa, Antarctica, Australia, South America, and India were joined in a supercontinent known as Gondwana. Near its heart lay Madagascar. The earth's climate was tropical then; dinosaurs roamed the land; and the first primitive mammals, small and nocturnal, had recently appeared. Then Gondwana began to break up. Madagascar separated from the east coast of Africa and eased away into the ocean, carrying a cargo of life from the age of dinosaurs—Gondwana's Ark.

More than 40 million years ago, some amazing new visitors came ashore. Madagascar was closer to Africa then; the sea level was lower; and a few creatures from the continent drifted over to the island. All were natives of the tropical forests that then covered much of Africa, and all were compact and hardy enough to crouch inside a hollow log or cling to a raft of debris swept across the shallow seas to Madagascar. They were mammals, the heirs to the post-dinosaur world, but only a few made the passage: There were tiny rodents and hedgehoglike insectivores; early carnivores related to the mongoose; and ancestral lemurs, the first members of the order known as primates.

Madagascar moved farther east, forever stranding the new immigrants on the island. Elsewhere in the world, the same species that came to Madagascar evolved into different forms to compete with other creatures that developed on the continents and crossed the land bridges between them. By 35 million years ago, the ancestral lemurs that once thrived across North America, Europe, and Africa were replaced by a new group of primates. They were anthropoids, the ancestors of monkeys, apes, and humans. Their brains were bigger, and perhaps because of their more competitive societies, the ancient lemurs—members of the prosimian primate branch—gradually disappeared. In Africa and Asia today the only surviving descendants are bush babies and lorises—small prosimians that endured in a world of anthropoids by remaining solitary and nocturnal.

As far as we know, no monkeys or apes ever reached Madagascar. Nor did predators like lions, hyenas, and jackals; four-legged grazers like antelopes—or even poisonous snakes. Several species of birds and bats flew to the island, and in the Pleistocene epoch of two million years ago, the crocodile and the pygmy hippopotamus swam over from Africa. With those exceptions, the animals that lived on Madagascar 40 million years ago had the island all to themselves.

The castaways flourished. Within its 227,000 square miles—an area larger than France—Madagascar holds the diversity of terrain and climate of a miniature continent. The animals adapted to rain forests, savannas, dry woodlands, and deserts, at altitudes ranging from sea level to nearly 10,000 feet. They mingled with survivors from the dinosaur age: giant tortoises, boa constrictors, primitive frogs, and the magnificent elephant birds. Through the multimillion-year ages of isolation leading up to present times, some creatures remained basically unchanged, like living fossils, while others radiated in a panoply of fabulous forms unique to Madagascar.

Today, about 80 percent of the island's plants and animals occur nowhere

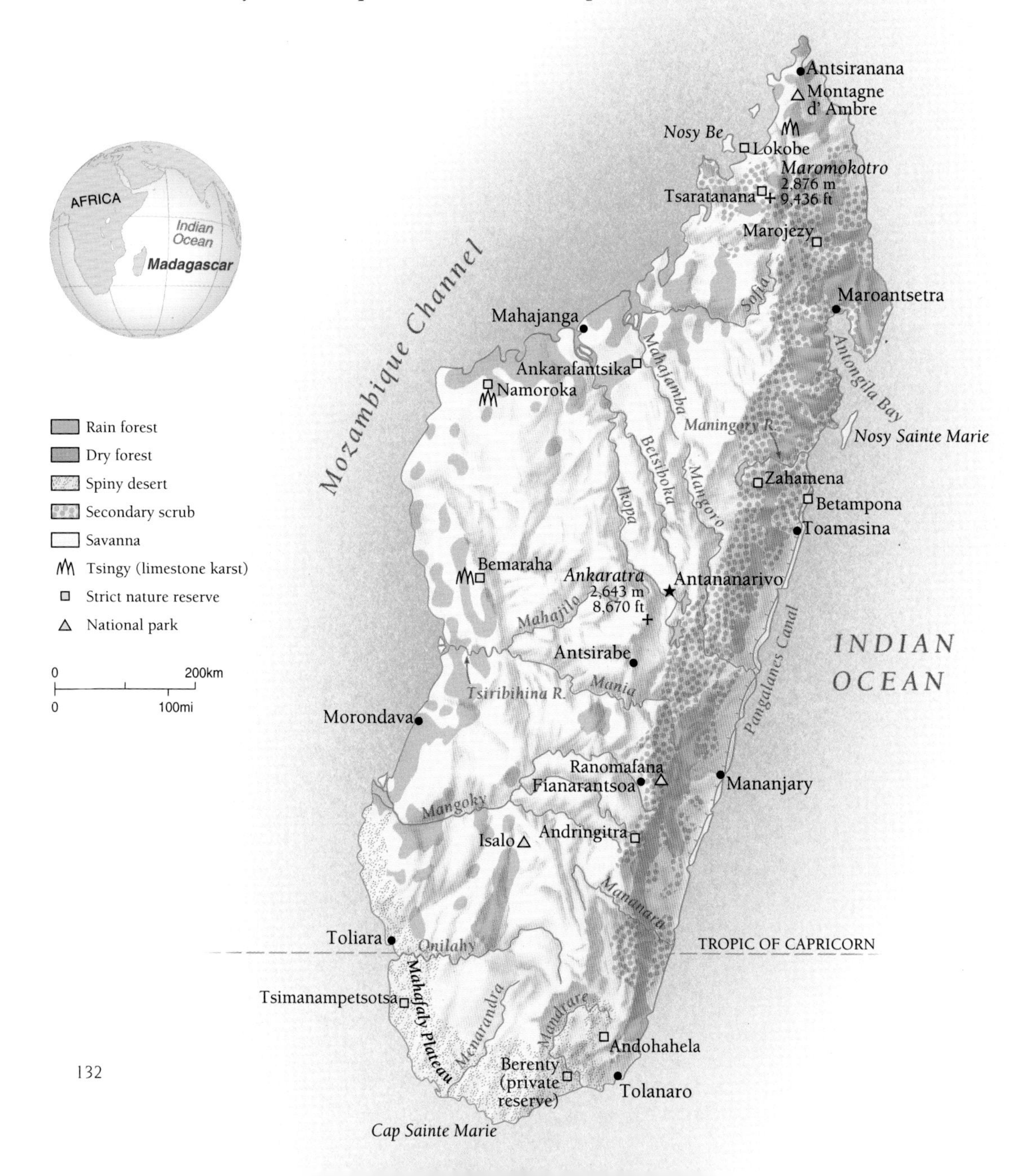

else on earth. Madagascar's 10,000 or more species of flowering plants account for one-fourth of the flora of the entire African region. Most of the island's 400 species of reptiles and amphibians are native to no other land. It is home to one-half of the world's chameleons, the charming lizards, with independently swiveling eyes, that change skin color according to mood. Even half of Madagascar's bird species are found only here, as are virtually all of its land mammals. Of the many strange forms in Madagascar's animal menagerie—from porcupine-spiked tenrecs to mongooses that prowl like panthers—the most wondrous of all are the lemurs. From their original seaborne ancestors, new lemurs arose in all shapes and guises, and in the absence of higher simian competitors, they made Madagascar a world of their own.

Just after sunrise in the rain forests of eastern Madagascar, an eerie melody rings through the trees. The song is silvery and haunting, first a lone cry that slides high up the scale, then descends in a fading, mournful wail. Other voices join in, liquid and clear, and replies chime from far off in the forest. Soon the thick, still air beneath the emerald canopy reverberates with unearthly harmonics, like the songs of whales in the sea. It is the music of the forests of Madagascar, sung by a lemur known as the indri. His face can be seen through the leaves, dark and furry with round ears like a teddy bear's and huge lemon-drop eyes. His mouth forms a rosy "O" when he tilts his head back to call. If you're near, his song pierces and chills. It is one of the loudest cries of any animal on earth, audible for more than two miles, but from a distance the tunes echo with a ghostly beauty, the melancholy voice of the forest primeval.

Rising up, the indri reveals his size. He's as big as a gibbon, with the lush black-and-white coat of a panda. Like other lemurs, he has opposable thumbs and toes for grasping; but unlike the others, he has no tail. Local people call him *babakoto*—cousin to man—and he's the largest lemur in the world.

A female clambers down the branch above him, and two younger faces appear over her shoulder. They might suddenly disappear now, but often they will stare down with more curiosity than fright—gathered pairs of yellow eyes gleaming in the greenery—then settle down to eat. Indris are vegetarian, and their diet of at least 70 species of fruits, leaves, and flowers is so complex that in captivity indris have never survived. They live in small family groups, communicating with other indris by song. Their lives seem languorous and unfettered: They sleep late, eat all day, retire early. In Africa, the diurnal niche for primates was usurped by monkeys and apes. Without them, the indris grew larger like the anthropoids and roamed free through the daylight hours. While it might seem that their cries and their tameness would give them away, adult indris

A*n alternate world survives on Madagascar, which broke away from the African continent some 160 million years ago. In isolation, its life-forms developed along a separate evolutionary path, and today 80 percent of the island's flora and fauna occur nowhere else.*

have no natural enemies and can sing without fear in the forests of Madagascar.

The variety of Madagascar's lemurs is like an evolutionary brainstorm of ideas. At least 11 other species share the rain forests with the indri, and a total of some 29 species live on the island. They constitute almost as many genera of primates as are found on the African continent, but here every one is a lemur. They range in size from the big fluffy indri to the tiny mouse lemur—the world's smallest primate, which can fit in the palm of your hand. There are lemurs of the forests and those of the desert; one lemur even hibernates. There are leaf-eaters, fruit-eaters, insectivores, and lemurs that feed on bamboo. There are monogamous red-bellied lemurs; and promiscuous troops of ringtails, the most terrestrial of the family, sometimes seen strolling in friendly gangs, their long raccoon tails pointed up like flagpoles.

As the indris begin to nod off to sleep, another creature awakens. High in a tree, a nest of twigs rustles, and a very weird hand reaches over the side. It has five digits with fingernails, and one is a thumb, but the four fingers are exceptionally long—and the middle one seems to belong to a skeleton. A head pops out, with orange owl eyes and great leathery, oversize ears like a bat's. Then the animal swings down and hangs by its feet, dangling a black ostrich-plume tail as it washes its dark, grizzled fur, performing its wake-up grooming.

It is an aye-aye, the most bizarre creature in all of Madagascar. As a whole it looks like no other living thing on earth. Its anatomy is so unusual that for about a century scientists could not agree on just what it was. Now classed as the sole member of its own family, Daubentoniidae, the aye-aye is also a lemur.

More than appearance sets the aye-aye apart. On Madagascar, some animals have taken the place of creatures that never reached the island. In a land without rabbits and squirrels or true rats and mice, Madagascar's seven unique genera of rodents arose to play their parts. Among the lemurs, the ringtail suggests Asia's macaque, and the mouse lemur replaces Africa's pygmy flying squirrel; but the aye-aye is the strangest of all: It's a mammal that acts like a bird.

Eyes wide, the aye-aye creeps out on a branch and slowly extends a hand. With its skeletal middle finger, it taps a fast tattoo on the bark and perks its ears forward to listen. It hears something and gnaws into the bark with teeth that are ever growing, like a beaver's, then reaches inside with the same thin finger to scoop out a meal of tender grubs. Tapping enables the aye-aye to detect changes in vibration that indicate insect galleries inside, and its sensitive ears pick up their movements. Excavating for larvae in trees, the aye-aye fills the niche of the woodpecker, a bird not found on Madagascar. It is also skilled at tearing into

Fishermen ply the coast in outrigger canoes like those that carried their ancestors to Madagascar.

coconuts, as a raccoon might do; in season, the aye-aye dines on hard-shelled nuts other animals can't crack, standing in for the role of squirrel. Though some people on Madagascar have long feared its startling appearance as a harbinger of death, the aye-aye, like other lemurs, is shy and inquisitive. It wanders around up in the trees, tapping and feeding through the night; then just before dawn, it slips back into its nest. Circling around inside like a house cat, it curls up in a ball, tail over its eyes, and sleeps.

About 4,000 years ago, sunrise around a lake in the central highlands of Madagascar lifted the curtain on a breathtaking stage of characters. The cast included lemurs and other mammals, reptiles, and birds—but many of them were giants. There were huge tortoises with four-foot-long shells grazing near the shore, pods of pygmy hippos sloshing in the water, and crocodiles that exceeded 20 feet in length basking along the banks. A dozen species of elephant birds roamed the surrounding grasslands, including the gargantuan *Aepyornis maximus*. There was a carnivore the size of a cougar that was a bigger version of his modern cousin, the fossa—a bobcat-size predator whose young resemble lion cubs, but which is not a cat at all, but a mongoose. Among them lived several species of giant lemurs. The biggest, *Megaladapis,* was the size of a female gorilla—and there was even a giant aye-aye.

Their home in the highlands was probably a mosaic of savanna and woodlands then. Some of the lemurs spent time in trees: *Megaladapis* shinnied up trunks like a koala to browse; *Palaeopropithecus* hung from boughs by all fours, sloth-style, as it munched on foliage. But some of the giant lemurs did something not many do today: They walked the land. A few were so large that they had to descend from the trees at times; other giant lemurs were primarily terrestrial. One species, *Archaeolemur,* may have traveled in troops like baboons, coming to the lakeshore to drink; another, *Hadropithecus,* was long-limbed and swift, and foraged for grass bulbs and seeds like early hominids in Africa. Around the highland lake in the alternate world of Madagascar, the ecological role of grazer and browser played by large hoofed mammals in mainland Africa was filled by tortoises, elephant birds, pygmy hippos, and lemurs. All the terrestrial lemurs but

The Ikopa River flows through terrain devoid of forest after centuries of environmental abuse.

one were bigger than the indri, and all of them began to vanish from the earth when one new primate reached Madagascar—and that was us.

Madagascar was one of the last large landmasses to be inhabited by humans. The ancestors of the Malagasy, the people of Madagascar, first reached the island nearly 1,500 years ago. Originally, they were Malayo-Polynesian people from the islands of Southeast Asia. They may have come from the island of Borneo, where some of their linguistic roots lie, then sailed across the Indian Ocean in outrigger canoes. They traveled the northern rim of the ocean basin via India and Arabia, then south down the African coast, and over to the shores of Madagascar. They carried a cultural heritage from two continents, a fusion found in their architecture, customs, and beliefs—and simply illustrated by their agricultural practices: They planted terraced rice fields like farmers in Asia and tended herds of zebu cattle they brought to Madagascar from Africa.

There is a Malagasy legend of an ancient fire that raged without end until it burned the center of the island down to its bones. The tale may represent a single conflagration, or it may be a collected memory of a long era of devastation. Either

On a freshly burned hillside, subsistence farmers plant rice.

way, the story is true. Evidence of fire is preserved in fossil sites, and deliberate burning continues even now. Most of Madagascar was once forested or lightly wooded. The people cleared the highland interior for paddies and burned off savanna woodlands for their livestock. Over the two millennia since their arrival, the Malagasy have drastically altered the face of the land. Seventy percent of the island is prairie now, and half of that is burned every year to create fresh pasture for cattle. Native vegetation now covers only 10 percent of the island. Madagascar has been so stripped of cover and gullied by rains that some say it is the most eroded land on earth. From the air, red clay soils show through thin vegetation like worn carpet. Madagascar is sometimes called the Great Red Island, and during the annual rains so much soil is bled from the land and flushed into the sea that astronauts from space have reported seeing a red ring around Madagascar.

It wasn't long after people arrived that Madagascar's megafauna began to disappear. Some biologists speculate that clearing and burning were to blame; others cite the overhunting of animals that had no defense against humans. It was surely both of those things—and something more insidious that leaves no evidence in the soils or fossil beds. The cattle and other domestic animals that came with the Malagasy were in direct competition with the native megafauna for grazing land and food. Against the new herds of hoofed mammals, the big native grazers died out.

Most of the recent destruction has taken place in the highlands that fill central Madagascar. Wilderness survives in pockets that encircle the perimeter of the island in what has been called a "necklace of pearls." Some of the pearls are parks; others are lands unsuitable for crops or herds; but a few remain untouched because they are almost impenetrable. Those are the pearls known as *tsingy,* the Malagasy word for "spikes." They are rugged massifs of stone, found in northern and western Madagascar. Each is an island castle, sheltering a sample of life from the land that surrounds it.

From the air, the tsingy of northern Madagascar looks like a medieval fortress—miles of gray limestone spires pointed up like spears. They rise more than 100 feet tall, and when tapped with a rock, they ring like the sound of their Malagasy name. They are sharp enough to impale and dangerous to cross, but if you watched long enough, you might see a crowned lemur bound with ease across the pinnacles, leaping gracefully from point to point, then disappear. There's another world down in the pinnacles, a mini-Madagascar within the island itself, and the lemur is heading there.

Below the stone ramparts there are sunken forests and pools, caves with underground rivers, and creatures that have never known humans. There are troops of crowned lemurs with gray caps and rufous face bands, and pretty Sanford's lemurs, whose males sport a white head fringe. At night fat-tailed dwarf lemurs appear, along with others called avahis—and the sleek fossa, which will stalk any small creature it can find. There are two species of Madagascar's unique tenrec family here, the hedgehog impersonators that waddle around the forest floor looking for insects. They roll into sea-urchin balls when threatened and communicate with one another in the gloom of the forest by supersonic vibrations of their quills. By day there are bright geckos among the leaves, including the lime-green-and-orange *Phelsuma* and the multicolored chameleons, which creep along branches with slow-rocking steps to zap insects with their long, sticky tongues. Underneath the pinnacles are caves the size of cathedrals and sunless waters where blind white fish prey on blind white shrimp, and huge crocodiles glide in the dark.

Farther south, the tsingy of the western dry forest is even more forbidding. Tall ranks of sharp peaks rise from a limestone plateau that covers more than 500 square miles. Few have ventured far inside. The dry forest around and within the spired plateau is the heartland of Madagascar's massive baobabs—the trees that seem to grow upside down. Though baobabs are often viewed as hallmark trees of mainland Africa, only one species lives there. Australia has one baobab as well, but Madagascar, with six species, may be their original home, and the baobab's spread to the other continents may date to the time when the lands were connected, in the ancient days of Gondwana.

Baobabs and other dry forest plants have evolved strategies to cope with eight months of drought each year. Some have thick, fleshy leaves or swollen trunks that store water; many trees are deciduous, dropping their foliage for the rainless months that are the tropic equivalent of winter. Even the tiny fork-marked lemurs that live here have a survival trick: They are biologically adapted to digest gum secreted by the trees, and it helps sustain them through the long dry months without fruits or leaves to eat. Red-fronted lemurs and snow-white sifakas have also been sighted here, but the tsingy is so huge and labyrinthine and little explored that no one is certain what else may live within its spires.

Even beyond the tsingy, Madagascar has entire mountains and river basins that have not felt the footsteps of scientists. Recently, worldwide conservation efforts have focused on the island, but the cutting and burning of forest continues. The population of Madagascar has more than doubled in the past 25 years and is still rising fast. Most people are subsistence farmers and fishermen, and while many realize what is being lost, people must feed their families.

Even as virgin forest is felled, new species of plants—and even animals—are found every year. Two new genera of palms have been recently identified, and in the southwestern desert a zoologist discovered a new species of mongoose previously represented by mislabeled specimens locked away in museum drawers. Entomologists find more than they have time to classify. Like everything else on the island, Madagascar's insects are unique. There are more than 800 species of moths and butterflies, including one that is merely speculated to exist because of a clue from a plant: Madagascar has a rare native orchid that could only be pollinated by a moth with a tongue 15 inches long, but the moth has never been seen.

Several varieties of bamboo grow in the eastern rain forest, and two species of lemurs were known to consume them. One, the greater bamboo lemur, was long believed to be extinct until 1964, when a naturalist spotted one in a village market, destined for a cook pot. He purchased the lemur, but it escaped, and eight years passed before he discovered a troop of its kin, living on a coffee plantation. In the mid-1980s, primatologists renewed the search for more greater bamboo lemurs. They thought they had found one when they spied a big red lemur with golden eyebrows and cheeks, crunching on a stalk of bamboo. More appeared, but as the scientists watched them, something seemed wrong. Greater bamboo lemurs traveled in small families and made raucous calls; these formed large groups, and they purred. They later realized that this purring lemur was completely unknown. It is now called *Hapalemur aureus,* the golden bamboo lemur, and its discovery would be sensational anywhere in the world: It is a new species of primate.

In the spiny desert of southern Madagascar, midwinter has passed, and the sun shines a bit longer each day. The swollen *Pachypodiums* and baobabs with their roots-up silhouettes have long since lost their spring leaves, as have the spiked clumps and thorny mazes of *Didierea*—cactus look-alikes with the woody stems of trees. It is the height of the dry season now, and all of them are blooming. They spangle the desert with red, white, and yellow—flowering now so that their seeds will set when the rains return.

In the boughs of a thorned tree by the sandy creek, the sifaka troop perches in the sun, eating blossoms. Tiny faces peer over the shoulders of the females. Like all lemurs, the sifakas raise their newborns to wean during the rainy season, when fresh greenery appears for the young ones. The sun climbs high, stirring heat from the surface of the desert. It wavers up, conjuring a mirage of a land from the age of Gondwana. It shimmers through plants not yet given words to name them, which have grown there for uncounted time, on an island that still has eyes unmet in the forests, and wingbeats unheard. The sifakas rise up and spring off and away, until they disappear on the horizon like shooting stars. Below, in the sandy creek bed, a fossil bone glints white in the sun.

Like monuments of a bygone time, baobabs—leafless in a winter

sunset—rise above a dry forest near Morondava.

In Madagascar, the aye-aye became a symbol to me of all that's weird, wonderful, and misunderstood about this remarkable island. With its skeletal middle finger, an aye-aye (opposite) spoons out coconut meat through a hole dug in the husk with its ever growing teeth. On the forest floor, I found another bizarre resident. The spiny tenrec, which some say is a cousin of early mammals long vanished from the earth, still holds its own in the isolation of Madagascar.

A russet-colored ring-tailed mongoose (opposite), one of Madagascar's eight indigenous carnivores, stares at me before it slips into the understory of the eastern rain forest. Sucker feet and frills along the length of its body help the leaf-tailed gecko (below) stay still on tree trunks and remain hidden. Like virtually all of Madagascar's reptiles, it is found nowhere else on earth.

FOLLOWING PAGES: *An impenetrable fortress of limestone pinnacles one hundred feet high shields pockets of forest from human intrusion.*

Crowned by a green inflorescence, an aloe rises out of the

spiny desert of the Mahafaly Plateau.

Roaming with lemurs through a southern forest, I fell under the spell of the subtle rhythms of their daily lives. Sifakas, such as these two sitting droopy-eyed in a tamarind (opposite), like to wedge inside a fork for a midday siesta. For a young ringtail clinging to its mother, noontime breaks—when the whole troop comes together—are a time to look around for playmates.

Few sights in the forests of Madagascar are as arresting as a gang of ringtails rushing across an open area with tails raised high and fluffy. Their long tails are essential for keeping balance while the ringtails run or leap between trees; but these primates, which are intensely social creatures, also use their strikingly marked tails for communication.

To some they're little dragons, evoking a distant past, but to me chameleons appear more like they've escaped from an imaginary future world. Their amazing physiology includes independently swiveling eyes; color changes that mirror emotional stress; and clasping feet that are moved ever so slowly, one at a time. More than 30 species of chameleons —over half of the world's total—have already been described in Madagascar, and more probably await discovery.

Unafraid of humans after years of protection, a pair of sifakas perch near a worker's cabin at Berenty, *a private reserve in southern* Madagascar. *A fruiting tree too far away to reach in a single leap prompts another sifaka to hop across a clearing.*

OKAVANGO

The Gift of a River

There is no better way to witness Okavango's animal life than to crouch down at a water hole in the dry season. By returning day after day, I became a fixture in the landscape; herds of elephants and antelopes took little notice of me as they came to slake their thirst. Tension filled the air one morning when four lionesses (overleaf), hungry after a night of failed hunting, stared into my lens as they drank. In a marsh near the delta, I watched zebras (following pages) bolt at a danger imagined, and panic rippled through their ranks as they fled.

A *bullfrog guards a pool of rainwater that just weeks before was a bone-dry pan.*

Awaiting the Return of the Rain

The wind picks up. It swirls the dust on the surface of the pan, gusts waves through the grasslands, rocks the trees. To the north, a high, bruised thunderhead spreads across the horizon on great dark wings. Beneath them, lightning bolts shoot down, flickering the clouds like strobes, releasing splintering booms as the storm races toward the pan. The soil is cracked and powdery after a year of baking sun, but now the storm skies rush near and lower as if to touch the earth, carrying the electric smell of rain. Heavy drops splatter into the dust, and then the clouds break. The rain falls in torrents, roaring down with the sound of a thousand drums. In this dry heartland of southern Africa, the season of rains comes as a benediction, but the first storm arrives like an elemental expression of ecstasy, a wild beat that summons the earth.

Deep beneath the pan a bullfrog rests, burrowed in the hard clay, encased in a thin membrane that protects him from drying. His eyes are closed tight; he is in suspended animation. He may estivate like this for a year, perhaps longer, but his entire life hinges on the moment of the rains. When they come, softening the earth around him, he works his way up to the surface, to the pan that is now a blue pool of fresh water. There he claims a new territory and calls out for a mate, eyes open on a brief new world.

The tiny pool that is his kingdom gleams near the center of a vast sand basin that fills the interior of southern Africa, extending from the Orange River of South Africa more than 1,500 miles north to the Congo, the largest stretch of sand in the world. In places the sands reach depths of a thousand feet, their great beds eroded and ground from the uplands of ancient Africa some 80 million years ago. The basin is known as the Kalahari, "the great thirstland" to the Afrikaners who trekked across it in the 1800s, a last refuge to the Bushmen who have roamed there for tens of thousands of years. At their deepest, broadest, and driest, the Kalahari sands reach across northern Namibia to Zimbabwe and extend south to cover most of Botswana, a country nearly the size of Texas, landlocked in the heart of southern Africa. The Kalahari makes much of Botswana a desert but for one remarkable place not far from the frog's pool: the Okavango Delta, a mighty swamp in the midst of the sands that creates a glorious oasis of life.

The Okavango is the world's largest inland delta, the gift of a river whose waters flow into the desert and never reach the sea. It spreads out in a fan across 8,500 square miles of Kalahari sands in northern Botswana. Within sprawls a wetland world of papyrus swamps, palm islands, and winding channels of crystalline water; around and beyond lie miles of savanna woodlands, desert flats, and salt pans. Across this region roams a nation of wildlife that includes creatures from lions and wild dogs, kudus and sitatungas, to elephants numbering as many as 65,000—the largest free-ranging herds in the world. In a continent where increasing human population, poaching, and political instability have devastated wild places and wildlife, Botswana's Okavango region stands apart, long ignored in its remote desert isolation and left largely intact in a stable country moving cautiously with its resources. The Okavango is a crown jewel of African wilderness. It holds one of the last great assemblages of the continent's

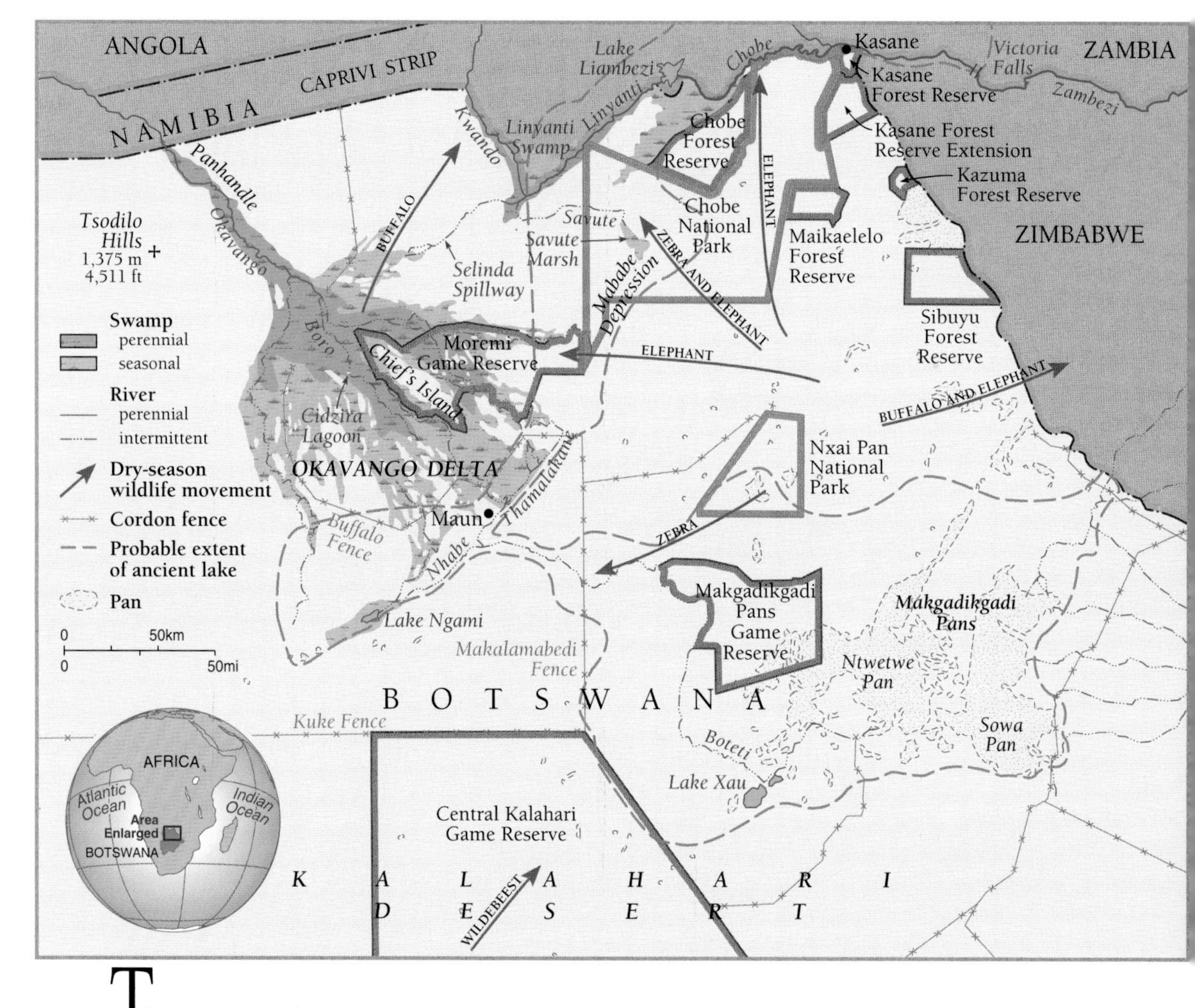

The Okavango Delta covers 8,500 square miles of northern Botswana. Annual rains from the Angola highlands feed the Okavango River and swell the delta. As the floods wane, local rains replenish the swamp. Across the region, wildlife responds to the seasonal rhythms of water.

wildlife that has a chance of surviving into the next century—and a delicately linked system of land-and-water worlds that together present a wondrous vision of Africa primeval.

Water is the lifeblood of the land, and like the frog that emerges from the earth, the Okavango owes its existence to the rains—but from storms that break in a faraway place. Away and up in the highlands of Angola, about a thousand miles northwest of the delta, fresh springs bubble up from the mile-high Benguela Plateau and trickle down the slopes, gathering into streams that join to form a river, the Cubango. Each year, heavy rains in the Angola highlands fill the river with a fresh surge of water as it flows south across lowland plains, broadening as it runs southeast through Namibia's Caprivi Strip and into northern Botswana. There the river, now called the Okavango, crosses a fault—a gentle drop—and spreads its waters like a great hand outstretched, creating the Okavango Delta. The annual rains from the highlands travel the river and through the delta in a wave of water that rolls through the fanning channels, spills over into swamplands and floodplains, and ripples out to the delta's very fingertips. Here at the Okavango's outermost reaches, another fault, a slight shift up, prevents the waters from seeping farther. So vast is the delta's size and so subtle the topographical changes that form it that the Angola rains may take as long as six months to flow from their highland source to the farthest edges of the delta, where the last of the river waters melt into the sands of the Kalahari.

Every creature in the great ark of wildlife that inhabits the Okavango lives by the rhythms of the waters. Seasonal movements, spawnings, nestings, births, and the seeding and blooming of the land are all timed to the pulse of the floods from Angola and the drumbeat of annual rains on the delta. The rains and floodwaters come and go in an elegant alternating synchrony: As the floods from Angola wane and the delta waters recede to their lowest ebb, the local rains arrive to replenish the swamp and soak the land, and as the wet season ends and the surrounding lands dry out, the floods return to roll through the delta.

High in a tree above a delta lagoon, a fish eagle throws its head back and screams. Against the surrounding dark greenery, its white chest shines like a lantern. With first light its cries echo over the waters, the haunting reveille call of the Okavango swamp. As the sun climbs, the eagle flaps off and circles up to soar on thermals above the delta, scouting for fish. High aloft it is king of the African skies, but earthbound it must defend its hunting rights. With the ebb and flow of the floods, fish eagle territories contract and expand, and each year as the floodwaters fall, the great birds fight for their shrinking domains in wild aerial battles, plummeting from the skies, locked talon to talon, heads arched back, as they scream out their claims to the delta.

The eagle spirals up, eyeing the immense green tapestry of the swamp, laced with blue channels, sequined with sunlight. Beyond the waters and floodplains stretch dry savannas that yield in the distance to long expanses of sandy scrubland and, farther out, to blinding white salt pans. Each is a part of the grand interlocking kingdom of the Okavango, linked one to the next by the intricate paths of water and wildlife leading into and out from the delta.

At the core lies the permanent swamp, where hippos grunt and crocodiles lurk in wetlands lush with vast fields of papyrus and phragmites, and sprinkled with archipelagoes of round palm isles. Beneath the islands labors a secret architect of Okavango geography. It is one of the swamp's more diminutive residents—the lowly termite, a creature of the soil whose underground colonies form the earthly foundation upon which some of the isles of the delta arise. On still, humid evenings when the rains first begin, tiny cracks appear in the termite mounds, and suddenly millions of winged young pour out and take flight over the delta in brown, smoky swarms. Frogs, snakes, lizards, and birds feast on the tumbling clouds of insects, but it takes only one surviving termite pair to burrow in and begin a new colony. As the surrounding plains dry after the rains have passed, new mounds appear like bubbles on the land. Built of a mixture of clay, salt, and sand, they are cemented, grain by grain, with termite saliva, making them resistant to erosion and moisture. Over time a mound slowly grows. Its base broadens; craggy fingers and spires rise up. Seasonal floods sweep sediments against the base; birds perch on top, dropping seeds, and soon, grasses and trees take root. From a termite castle that looms up from the swamp and may shelter an active colony for as long as 80 years, a new island is born in the delta—and the water curves gently around it.

Submerged in the cool of lagoons and quiet channels, the Okavango's most massive water resident rearranges the delta's geography in a bolder way. Flattening stands of grasses as it comes ashore to graze, wallowing in mud pots and pools, barging through reed jams in waterways, the mighty hippopotamus rears up from the water and roars, teeth bared, then lumbers up to land, leaving a soggy path of deep prints into which water seeps, then eventually flows. Sometime, long after the hippo has passed, a stream may divert into its trail, creating a fresh passage through the swamp.

Although predators like lions and hyenas can swim between isles if they must, the innermost delta is largely a haven for the few big animals equipped for life in a watery prairie. Of Africa's more than 70 species of antelope, one is uniquely adapted to the heart of the swamp: the shy and solitary sitatunga. From the water-level view of a dugout canoe, the inner delta presents serpentine tunnels of nodding papyrus, but if you could wing up like an eagle, you might spy, in a small clearing in the stands of swamp grasses, a sitatunga resting in the afternoon light. He resembles a big bushbuck, and his horns spiral back like a kudu's, but his niche in the delta is secured by his hooves: They are long and deeply cloven, with flexible ankle joints that permit them to splay, distributing his weight and enabling him to bound with ease across soupy beds of reeds. His hooves give him access to grazing other antelope can't reach, and an odd sound that may be heard deep in the delta at dusk is the popping of papyrus as the sitatunga snaps the tall stalks to feed on the tender crowns.

Hovering low, you might hear a soft rustle on a nearby isle as a lioness eases toward the water and freezes. The sitatunga starts. Alarmed, he bolts through the reeds and leaps into a channel, legs pedaling fast. He swims hard across the water, then dives into a secluded cove, where he remains motionless, waiting until danger has passed, completely submerged but for the tips of his nostrils.

As the Okavango waters recede to their lowest ebb, masses of birds arrive to nest in the delta. Some move in from the surrounding lands, while others travel from distant points in Africa, joining wintering flocks that come from as far away as Europe and the Middle East. African skimmers migrate in from the north

A herd of red lechwes races across flooded grasslands on the edge of the delta.

to lay their eggs on exposed sandbars; masked weavers build hanging nests in the reeds; and carmine bee-eaters bore colonial nesting burrows in riverbanks as the water level drops. Sacred ibises, egrets, spoonbills, and several species of herons and storks nest communally on islets of water figs rooted in the swamp shallows. Each species occupies a discrete layer in the fig thickets, their downy chicks peering out from different levels in the scrub like passengers on the decks of a riverboat—in nests just high enough up from the water to be safe from the snap of a crocodile.

The crocodiles themselves nest on lands exposed by the falling waters, their eggs incubated by the ever higher sun of the Kalahari summer. Like the bird chicks that must fledge before the floods rise again, the young crocodiles must hatch in time, or drown. From inside their eggs, baby crocodiles ready to emerge call out with muffled squeals that at times can be heard more than 50 feet away. If necessary, a female will dig up her clutch and carry the hatchlings off to safety in her mouth; even male crocodiles have been known to roll eggs around on their tongues to help the young break out before the floods.

It comes in silence, like the tide. The surge from Angola flows south. It fills the narrow panhandle of the Okavango River and eases over the banks, seeping across floodplains in a shimmering sheet, making the grasslands shine. Over the fault, the flood fans out with the river and spreads through the braided channels of the swamp. It swells the veins of the delta, drowns the shores of the isles,

Oxbows of the Okavango River wind through papyrus swamp.

inches up and over the edges of every sinuous passage, trickling crooked wet paths through the sands.

Delta lagoons slowly rise. The china-white lilies that sprinkle the backwaters quiver with the incoming current. Then their heart-shaped pads begin to turn like wheels as their stems, coiled underwater, untwist to reach up with the flood. In deeper channels the waters rush fast, breaking through dams of dead grasses, flooding underground burrows, flushing out swirls of insects, and sweeping tons of detritus, nutrients, and seeds through the delta and out to the floodplains. Dark streams of fish—African pike, climbing perch, and huge schools of barbels—race out with the waters to spawn on freshly flooded lands, pursued by circling eagles, hovering kingfishers, and high-stepping storks, staring intently into the shallows as they follow the advance of the water.

Though few people live in the inner reaches of the Okavango, news of the coming of the flood travels faster than rumor from the villages high up the river to those along the farthest fringes of the swamp. The news moves in more mysterious ways among the great herds of animals spread far and wide through the savanna woodlands surrounding the delta. Thousands of the big mammal nomads of the land—thundering herds of buffaloes, wildebeests, and zebras; bounding troupes of antelopes; loping bands of giraffes; and tribes of elephants roaming like shifting gray hills—seem to raise their heads to the wind and catch the scent of the flood.

To the edges of the swamp come the herds. They trek in from afar on worn trails that crisscross the woodlands, radiating out from every water hole like rays of the sun, connecting every pool and pan in the land, and leading finally to the swamp. Here, along the delta's edge, gather the richest concentrations of animals in the Okavango. They come for the rush of fresh water and the flush of green grasses that sprout from the plains as the flood seeps across. The herds travel in and out from the woodlands to feed on the new growth and to drink from the delta, moving deeper toward the permanent swamp as the months pass, following the retreating line of the flood.

The seasonal movements of the animals tie the inner delta to the lands beyond, and at the boundary of every habitat in the Okavango region, it seems there's a species of antelope to bridge the gap, from swamp to floodplain to woodland to desert. Graceful herds of red lechwes live with the flux of the floodplain, subsisting on grasses of the delta's moving edge. Even their larger life cycles follow the rhythms of the flood. The lechwe herds mate before the waters rise. As if in natural measure of the flood's increase, the females grow fat

The Buffalo Fence forms a barrier between the delta and the livestock land beyond.

as the delta swells and give birth as the receding waters provide a sweet flush of grass for their newborn.

Peering out from the delta woodlands at night shine the eyes of impalas, the balletic antelope beauties of the border country where savanna merges into trees, their eyes twinkling white, at shoulder height, in the moving beam of a flashlight. If you pan a light in the dark across the grasses and boughs, the bush will sparkle with the eyes of the night. The animals are revealed by their place in the land and by the size, color, and certain gleam of their eyes—golden orbs for the bush babies high in the trees, red for the hyenas, skulking low, and bouncing white balls for the springhares, hopping out from their burrows to feed in the cover of darkness. But the herd of impalas gazing out through the trees, eyes clustered together in a starry constellation, is watching for one particular animal—the lioness whose eyes glint like orange mirrors in a beam of light as a pride of hungry females fans out in formation to hunt.

The lionesses drop down, slinking low on soft paws, stalking now in a silent, invisible crescent, closing in on the twinkle of eyes. But the impalas have seen them. One barks like a cough—a warning. Across the scrub, another barks back, and the alarm sounds through the bush in a zigzagging relay of calls. The lionesses rush out—then halt, foiled as the impalas bound off in a wild flurry of leaps. Springing in jumps that can cover 30 feet, the impalas secrete puffs of scent from glands in their heels that may guide the herd along the same path of flight in the melee of escape through the dark and thick of the bush.

This night the lionesses fail, but on another, they won't. Though in the final moments of the hunt they may slip from view—so swift and sudden is their ambush—you'll find them eventually, perhaps guided by the whoop of hyenas circling in the shadows of the kill, watching, as the lionesses feed, for a chance to move in and feast.

While impalas will only step out from the security of the trees to drink from the delta when they must—getting extra moisture from woodland browse and dew—the buffaloes and wildebeests survive on dry grasses and must ever move on in search of water, trudging through the seasons over the changing mosaic of the delta, in to the waters of the flood and out to the temporal pools of the rains. Their meandering paths twine with those of other wanderers to form the threadbare trails that weave through the lands of the Okavango.

The dry season deepens as the floodwaters fall. The days grow longer, temperatures rise. By mid-morning, mirages waver up like steam and the air throbs with heat. Fickle winds twirl dust into powdery funnels that skip over the plains and into the woodlands, spinning fallen leaves into mad, rising whorls, only to stop, of a sudden—like the end of a breath. Even the animals seem restless, impatient for relief from the withering land. Female buffaloes, wildebeests, zebras, and impalas, which will give birth after the annual rains arrive, move slowly now, bellies heavy with young. Lone bull elephants roaming the woodlands seem edgy, knocking down trees they have no need to eat. The temper of the land is frayed; all life awaits the rains.

In the sear of the noonday sun, mopane leaves fold like wings, and as their seeds fall—sticky whirligigs lofted by winds—some cling to the coats and hooves of animals that carry them into the delta and spread them out over the land. It's humid now, and thick, though above the sky stretches endlessly blue. Then, like a sign of faith in what has always been promised, as if in ancient understanding that the rains will come, many savanna bushes and trees, at the desperate height of the dry season, burst into bloom.

In the tense months before the rains arrive, families of elephants in ever increasing herds converge on the waters of northern Botswana, sometimes arriving on the run to reach the waters they must drink regularly to survive. They gather around the edges of the delta and eastward along a network of fugitive streams and smaller swamps connecting the Okavango to a river called the Chobe. They come from hundreds of miles around, from the drying lands surrounding the delta and from other countries to the north and east. Here in northern Botswana the grandest animals of all Africa find haven in greater numbers than in any other place on the continent. Their prodigious presence speaks to a hard reality. The elephants come not only for the water but also because they know they are safe—an understanding evidenced by the flight of elephants elsewhere in Africa into the protected lands of parks. Their knowledge of human boundaries is poignantly demonstrated by a specific thing the elephants do when they congregate along the Chobe River in Botswana. Across the river lies the Caprivi Strip of Namibia, a place where elephants have been heavily poached, but where the shores are lush with grasses and trees. From the Botswana side of the Chobe, the elephants swim to Namibia, submerged in the river, trunks up like periscopes for air. They often cross over at dusk, to graze and browse in the cover of darkness, then swim back in the hours of dawn to the refuge of Botswana.

In the Okavango, and wherever they mass in great numbers, elephants physically alter the land, sometimes battering down stands of trees to feed on the bark and leaves, changing whole landscapes from woodlands to open savannas. Homing in on trees heavy with ripening fruit, they feast and move on, spreading seeds in the fertilizing medium of their dung to distant places where new forests may someday arise in the wake of their passing. Even in subtle ways, their movements affect the lives of other creatures, which feed on the foods they knock down from on high and follow the trails they make in the bush. In the delta, the elephants wade far into the swamp, plowing freshwater trails through the grass, and from the savanna woodlands surrounding the Okavango they have tramped paths that angle southeast across the long flats of Kalahari sands. If you look down from the sky, you can see the elephants' routes—wide trails that lead to what was once a mighty expanse of water. Their paths trace a course to the edge of a huge, dry lake bed known as the Makgadikgadi Pans. Extending over an area of 15,000 square miles, they are the largest salt pans in the world, white like bones bleached in the African sun, empty now of all but mirage.

In a wetter era of ancient Africa some two million years ago, the Okavango,

Chobe, and Zambezi Rivers all flowed down into southeast Africa's Limpopo River and out to the Indian Ocean. Then an upheaval in the earth created a fault line that blocked the three rivers from reaching the Limpopo, and their waters ponded back into the great depression of Makgadikgadi, forming a superlake that covered some 23,000 square miles. The earth shifted again, and the Chobe and Zambezi turned east, their waters joining together to plunge in a spectacular cascade over Victoria Falls, leaving the Okavango behind to flow alone into the basin of the Kalahari.

For a time, Makgadikgadi was linked to the Okavango Delta. When the floodwaters from Angola reached the fingertips of the swamp, they flowed into a narrow river, the Boteti, that leads down to Makgadikgadi. The floodwaters filled the depression, and great numbers of animals came down from the Okavango and in from the Kalahari to the great shining lake in the desert. But as the climate grew drier, the Makgadikgadi slowly evaporated. Its shrinking size is marked by ever smaller concentric rings of old shoreline ridges—recent enough that the tools and spearpoints of early humans may be found there, where the waters once lapped and they crouched to hunt.

Although the waters of the Boteti almost never reach the pans now, in unusual years—perhaps once a decade—heavy rains fall on the Makgadikgadi and fill the old lake bed with a thin sheet of water. Then, from hundreds of miles around, antelopes and birds flock to the pans. Springboks and gemsboks come in from the desert, and herds of wildebeests, zebras, and even elephants travel down from the Okavango. The new waters teem with uncounted billions of brine shrimp, whose eggs lie dormant within the cracked pans, where they may rest for years until the arrival of the rain that brings them to life. Fleets of white pelicans swoop down from the delta, and from other places in Africa—no one is certain just where—tens of thousands of flamingos wing in to the pans, somehow possessed of a knowledge that the lake has reappeared. Within days the shallows are blanketed pink, murmuring with the sound of flamingos, the perfect emblem of the Makgadikgadi, their presence as ephemeral as the very existence of the waters. Packed in dense flocks, the flamingos court and dance, feasting on the shrimp and building mound nests for their eggs far out in the pans. As the Makgadikgadi dries out and the young ones fledge, the flamingos move off in pink clouds into the African skies, to destinations as mysterious as those from which they came.

The animals that have journeyed to the pans slowly disappear, the springboks and gemsboks dispersing into the deserts, while the wildebeests, zebras, and elephants turn north, following trails their generations have tracked into the sands of the Kalahari, leading back to the waters of the Okavango. The surrounding lands there have dried now, too, but the swamp shines blue, and under the clay of the small pan near the delta, the bullfrog lies burrowed again, awaiting the return of the rains.

From a friend's plane circling a few hundred feet above the delta, I looked out over hundreds of square miles of virtually intact wilderness (opposite). From my bird's perspective, I could see how the contours of the Okavango River are nearly lost in a labyrinth of islands and lagoons of the river's own making. All animals respond to the annual rising and falling of the water that flows from the Angola highlands. A yellow-billed stork (above) starts bringing nesting material back to a colony on an island deep in the delta when lowering water levels make fishing in isolated pools easier.

D*uring the dry season, elephants by the thousand gather*

around the delta from the surrounding areas.

When a herd of elephants came to drink from a water hole near the delta one dusty evening, I suddenly realized that the pace in the herd must be determined by the speed of the slowest animal. I watched a calf (below), only a few weeks old and still unable to suck water through its trunk, crouch down at the water's edge and try to drink with its mouth. Another day a lone bull (opposite) expressed displeasure at my proximity by flaring his ears and making a big splash. After months of almost daily contact with elephants, I could read their body language and sense a bluff, but periodically a serious charge would send the adrenaline rushing through my veins.

When I sank below the surface of the swamp (left), I saw for myself the miracle of its existence. Essentially the Okavango is just a *thin sheet of water stretched over the sands of the* Kalahari Basin. As I *plunged into the crystal water and eased to the bottom,* I *could see how the swaying pads of water lilies, afloat on the surface above me, were anchored in mere desert sand below.* Filtered *through endless beds of reeds and papyrus, the delta's water is so clear that most local people drink it straight from the swamp.*

Silent assassins that betray their movements with barely a ripple, crocodiles are rarely seen, but like most people I feared them. After

years of being hunted, only the most cunning crocs remain—those that have learned to keep a low profile in the delta's backwaters.

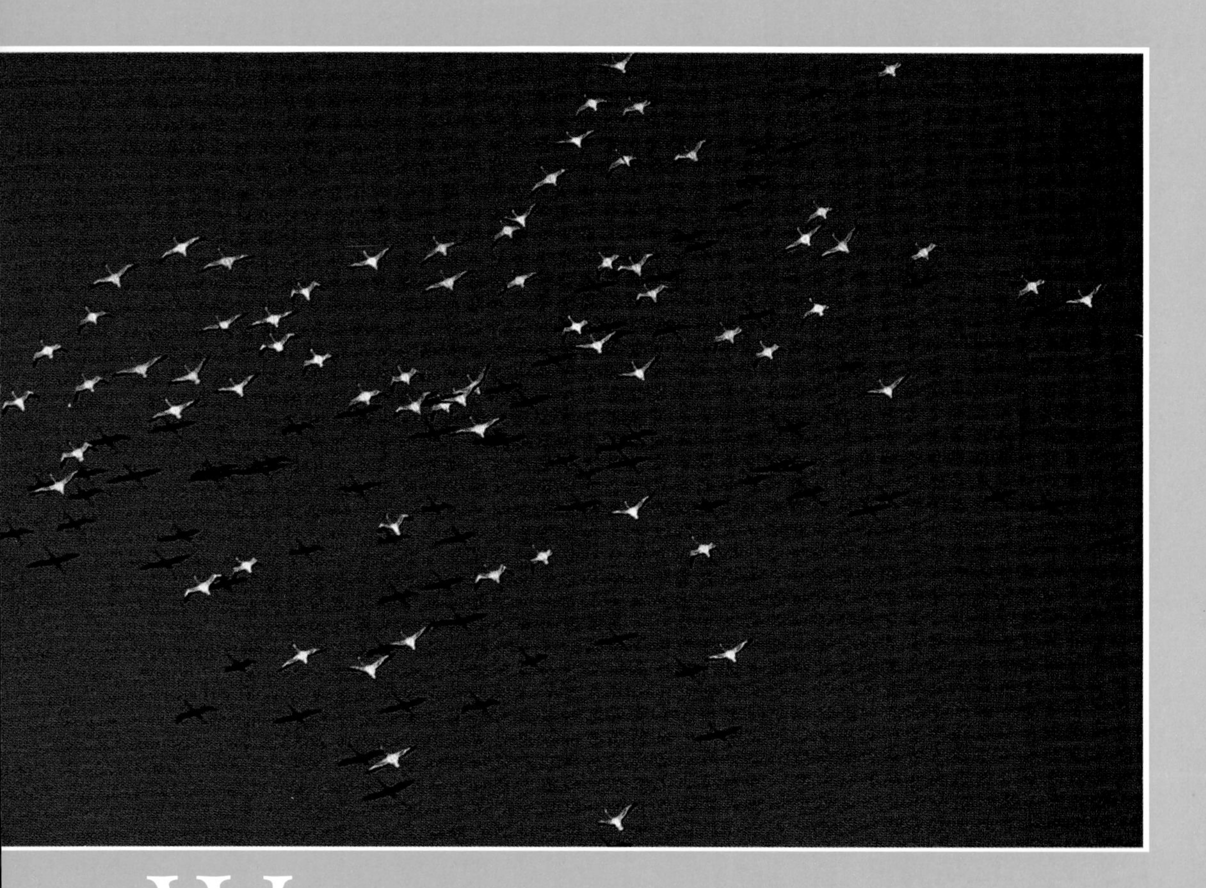

Whipped up by storm winds, briny foam streaks across the salt pans of Makgadikgadi *(opposite).* Once *a wetland like the* Okavango Delta, *the* Makgadikgadi *dried up in prehistoric times, when the river that fed it shifted course.* Today *the pans lie dry and lifeless for years at a time, but heavy rains occasionally re-create a temporary lake, which attracts many thousands of flamingos (above), lured from places thousands of miles away by clues as yet unexplained.* Everywhere *in the* Kalahari, *water precedes life.* Impalas *(preceding pages) give birth to their young shortly before the rainy season so that fawns can gain strength on tender green growth.*

Slinking forward from behind a termite mound, a lioness glances at antelopes in the open. She called off her hunt before it even began, having detected no weakness in her quarry nor a way to sneak up close for a surprise attack. Through millennia of natural selection, the predator's senses and those of its prey have been sharpened in an evolutionary race in which no one gains a permanent edge. Eyes and ears are closely matched; wits make the difference between life and death.

When the sun touches the horizon, there's a shift of characters on the African land. Buffaloes (below) emerge from cover and drift across the Chobe floodplains to graze through the coolness of the night. Teetering on a shaky platform at the edge of a bird rookery, I watched how young spoonbills (opposite), nearly full grown, eagerly awaited an evening meal from parents winging home, guided by the last light of day.

As an apprentice to a pride of lionesses, which took little offense at my presence, I roamed through the African night. Hunting, I learned, is a harsh way of life. Some nights we crisscrossed the darkened savanna for miles without ever getting close to game. Other nights it would be over quickly; a silent stalk followed by a short, spectacular chase, some muffled screams, and then contented grunts mixed with the crushing of bones. But even the awesome strength of lionesses was no deterrent for determined hyenas, which often succeeded in chasing the pride off their kill.

FOLLOWING PAGES: *Twilight comes to one of the last places in Africa large enough to contain the wanderlust of elephants and the memory of a world without man.*

On assignment in Borneo, writer Chris Eckstrom and photographer Frans Lanting pause for a portrait—briefly: Moments later they rescued Frans's unattended camera gear from an assertive orangutan. Before becoming a free lance in 1990, Chris worked as a National Geographic staff writer for 16 years, contributing chapters to numerous Society publications on subjects ranging from New England history to African wildlife. Over the past decade, Frans Lanting's award-winning photographs have appeared frequently in NATIONAL GEOGRAPHIC, as well as in many other of the world's leading magazines. His assignments in Madagascar and South Georgia received top honors from World Press Photo in 1988 and 1989; his Okavango coverage earned him the title of BBC Wildlife Photographer of the Year in 1991. When not traveling, Chris and Frans retreat to their home near Santa Cruz, California, in a coastal meadow they share with bobcats and coyotes.

A note from the authors: We would like to extend our sincere thanks and appreciation to the individuals, agencies, and organizations listed below, without whose assistance our work would not have been possible.

For each chapter, we have included books that will lead readers deeper into the subject. We have also listed addresses for local and international organizations that are active in the protection of these regions. We strongly urge readers with concern for the places we feature in this book to become involved in efforts to safeguard their survival.

Borneo

Louise Emmons and Clive Marsh (chief consultants), Tengku Adlin, Hamid Ahmad, Lamri Ali, Simon Ambi, Patrick Andau, Elizabeth Bennett, Ramesh "Zimbo" Boonratana, Simon Bosuong, Leo Chai, Terry Ko, Tony Lamb, Francis Liew, Wilfred Lingham, Jamili Nais, Junaidi Payne, Anthea Phillipps, Steve Pinfield, Noel Richard, Simon Sandi, Robert Stuebing; Danum Valley Field Centre, Sabah Foundation, Sabah Ministry of Tourism and Environmental Development, Sabah Parks, Sarawak Forests Department, Sarawak National Parks and Wildlife Office.

Suggested reading: *Wild Malaysia* by Junaidi Payne and Gerald Cubitt; *Borneo* by John MacKinnon; *Kinabalu: Summit of Borneo,* edited by Margaret Luping, Chin Wen, and E. Richard Dingley.

Conservation organizations:

Wildlife Conservation International
New York Zoological Society
Bronx, New York 10460

World Wide Fund for Nature Malaysia
WDT No. 40, 89400 Likas
Sabah, Malaysia

South Georgia

Peter Prince (chief consultant), Capt. Heinz Aye and the crew of the *Society Explorer,* the Chater family, the Poncet family, Werner Zehnder; Bird Island Field Station, British Antarctic Survey, British Armed Forces at Grytviken.

Suggested reading: *The Island of South Georgia* by Robert Headland; *Logbook for Grace* by Robert Cushman Murphy; *The Wandering Albatross* by William Jameson.

Conservation organizations:

International Council for Bird Preservation
32 Cambridge Road
Girton
Cambridge CB3 OPJ
United Kingdom

Falkland Conservation
Post Office Box 31
Port Stanley, Falkland Islands

Hawaii

Dave Boynton, Sherwin Carlquist, the late Harvey Fisher, Torrie Higashino, Jack and Gretchen Jeffrey, Brad and Annabelle Lewis, Susan Powell, Richard Voss; The Bernice P. Bishop Museum, Hawaii Department of Natural Resources, National Park Service, The Nature Conservancy, U.S. Fish and Wildlife Service, U.S. Geological Survey, U.S. Navy.

Suggested reading: *Hawaii: A Natural History* by Sherwin Carlquist; *Islands in a Far Sea: Nature and Man in Hawaii* by John L. Culliney; *Hawaii* by Robert Wallace.

Conservation organizations:

The Nature Conservancy of Hawaii
1116 Smith Street, Suite 201
Honolulu, Hawaii 96817

Sierra Club Legal Defense Fund
212 Merchant Street, Suite 202
Honolulu, Hawaii 96813

Madagascar

Alison Richard (chief consultant), Alison Jolly, Olivier Langrand, Bernhard Meier, Martin Nicoll, André Peyriéras, the late Georges Randrianasolo, Hubert Randrianasolo, Patricia Wright; Madagascar Department of Water and Forestry, Tsimbazaza Park, University of Madagascar, Antananarivo.

Suggested reading: *Madagascar: A World Out of Time* by Frans Lanting; *Madagascar: A Natural History* by Ken Preston-Mafham; *Madagascar: An Environmental Profile,* edited by M. D. Jenkins.

Conservation organizations:

Conservation International
1015 18th Street, N.W.
Washington, D.C. 20036

World Wide Fund for Nature
B.P. 738
Antananarivo, Madagascar

Okavango

Paul Sheller (chief consultant), the late Jack Bousfield, David Dugmore, Mike Gunn, Dereck and Beverly Joubert, Tim Liversedge, Tim and Bryony Longden, Ewan Masson, Susan Masson, Diane McMeekin, Elias Nkwane, Karen Ross, Lloyd and June Wilmot; Botswana Department of Wildlife and National Parks, Chobe Lion Research Camp, Ker, Downey and Selby, and Travel Wild.

Suggested reading: *Kalahari: Life's Variety in Dune and Delta* by Michael Main; *Okavango: Jewel of the Kalahari* by Karen Ross; *The Lost World of the Kalahari* by Laurens van der Post.

Conservation organizations:

African Wildlife Foundation
1717 Massachusetts Avenue, N.W.
Washington, D.C. 20036

Kalahari Conservation Society
Private Bag 28
Maun, Botswana

Library of Congress CIP Data
Eckstrom, Christine K.
Forgotten edens : exploring the world's wild places / photographic essays by Frans Lanting ; text essays by Christine K. Eckstrom ; prepared by the Book Division, National Geographic Society (U.S.).
p. cm.
Includes index.
ISBN 0-87044-866-8
1. Natural history. 2. Natural history—Pictorial works. I. Lanting, Frans. II. National Geographic Society (U.S.). Book Division. III. Title.
QH45.5.E25 1993
508—dc20 92-42371
CIP

Composition for this book by the Typographic section of National Geographic Production Services, Pre-Press Division. Set in Berkeley Book. Printed and bound by R. R. Donnelley & Sons, Willard, Ohio. Color separations by Graphic Art Service, Inc., Nashville, Tenn.; Lincoln Graphics, Inc., Cherry Hill, N.J.; and Phototype Color Graphics, Pennsauken, N.J. Dust jacket printed by Federated Lithographers-Printers, Inc., Providence, R.I.

Index